This Time Round
Copyright © 2015 Ray Quinn
All rights reserved.

Enquiries should be addressed to
Percy Publishing
Woodford Green,
Essex. IG8 0TF
England.

www.percy-publishing.com

1st Published March 2015
1st Edition
4th March 2015 1st Print
Chief Editor: Cherry Burroughs

ISBN: 978-0-9929298-7-9

Cover Design Copyright © 2014 Percy Publishing
Percy Publishing is a Clifford Marker Associates Ltd Company

Print: Svet Print, d.o.o., Ljubljana

Dedication

I'd like to dedicate this book in memory of my nan 'Margie' she'd tell me 'all you need is enough' I have it tattooed. But nan I want more. I love you and miss you dearly every day.

XXXX

I'd also like to thank two people, that have ran their life around me, loved me, cared for me and shown me how to be the best I can possibly be. I love you both very much Mum and Dad. Thank you for being the solid rock to come home to. Keeping my feet firmly on the ground, and being there for me no matter what. I couldn't live without you both in my life.

This Time Round

Introduction.

Most of you taking a look at this book will be people that over the years have watched me grow up on TV, from my teenage role in Brookside and then on X-Factor. Many of you will believe I've been very lucky in life, which in truth I have. What you may not know is that at some points it has been hard, harder than I ever would have imagined.

My story is going to take you on a journey - a journey that I have enjoyed - starting from my early years of dancing that many of you may not know about.

X-factor made me a household name, yes, but only at some cost to my happiness. My age had its price. Those around me used my age, naivety and my dream to be an entertainer to their own advantage. I'm not going to judge them. I'll just talk my way through my life and let you be the judge.

This book has been written so I can tell you my story, and despite the old saying 'You can't put old heads on young shoulders' maybe I can give a bit of a warning to anyone following their dream in the entertainment industry about the pitfalls of the life they aspire to.

If I could go back would I do things differently? Yes, I would. Do I regret my life? No, I don't.

This is my story and this is who I am now. I am closing a chapter and stepping towards a bright new horizon, and I would like to leave my past experiences behind me.

How you choose to interpret them is all up to you.

Chapter 1

Early Childhood Memories

I have always wanted to be an entertainer. It's in my blood - it's the way I'm wired up.

People have their own forte in life, be it as an athlete, businessman, scientist, politician or whatever. Mine is to perform.

I was born in 1988, the youngest of three sons by 18 years. From a young age I would dance in front of 'Top of the Pops' with my dummy microphone, or play guitar whilst performing for the family. I remember one of my favourite tracks at the time was 'Young at Heart' by the Bluebells. I would start singing and dancing - I just wanted everyone to watch me. My mum used to call me to let me know 'Top of the Pops' was on and I would be dancing about. The dog would be racing round after me and I'd be running around the slide that was in our lounge. (In those days we had to cross the road to get to our garden, so my mum put the slide in the lounge so I could play on it without being run over while going across.) I would copy all the songs word for word. Like my dad and brothers I was very much the attention seeker, but it was obvious I was not going down the same route in the flooring industry.

I didn't come from a family of entertainers already in the industry, albeit my dad was a natural entertainer in the local pub. He's a carpet fitter by trade and my two older brothers, our Robin and Darren, are also both carpet fitters; all the family are. My dad had taught my brothers and one day not long before I started college he said, "Come on! I'll give you a few quid for a day's work if you come and help me." I was doing a lot of dance and drama training at the time, Brookside had finished and I had nothing really on in the entertainment business. "It'll be good to learn a trade as you get older, something to fall back on. If you're skint you can always save yourself a few quid by fitting your own carpets." He was making a joke of it, but underneath I knew he was trying to make sure I didn't put all my eggs in one basket, which was fair enough as my dad has only ever had a trade and never stopped working.

When we got to the first place it was on the 7th bloody floor. The carpet was about 20-30 foot long, and it was massive to me as I was a tiny, scrawny little thing.

"Get the end there, Son!" my dad said. It was the best underlay money could buy at the time, really thick and heavy. My dad was in his fifties, but from a rugged Irish background, and he has always been strong and ready to go. He'd say "Come on Mate, give us a hand!" like it was nothing.

"Dad," I said, groaning back at him, "I can't lift it!"

"Just push it, Son! Go on, Lad!"

I couldn't do it, but I gave it everything I had and with a big struggle we managed to get it to the top of the stairs, and that was not even the job half done.

Then he said, "Right Son, now let's get the carpet!"

To which I replied, "Oh my God, Dad I can't!" and I knew from that moment there was no way I was going to be doing this for a living.

I used to look at my dad and brothers' hands and see they were always cut, rough and somewhat swollen; mine were soft and still are. The joke to this day in the family is that I have never lifted a hammer only a microphone! Our Robin and Darren could practically build their own houses, but I couldn't do anything like that even now. So what I gained from that experience was that it put me off manual labour for life. I suffered from meningitis as a baby, I was very ill and I was in hospital for three weeks and of course this was a very worrying time for my parents albeit that it has not really affected me. I think this is why my mum was very protective as I grew up.

In 1994 when I was six we had just moved from Knotty Ash, where we lived four doors away from Ken Dodd, when my mum took me to my first pantomime, 'Peter Pan the Lost Boys.' I remember we were four rows back from the front and I said, "I wanna do that, Mum". I was looking at the lads dancing around, acting and performing as the Lost Boys. "I wanna do that."

"Do what, Son?"

"Be like them, Mum!"

I longed to be on that stage, be that guy performing to an audience, and from that very day I guess my future was in my mum's hands.

***

At the age of three my mum had taken me to a dance studio called 'Millington's' that my brother Darren's now ex-wife recommended as she knew of it, and from what I gathered was friends with the owners at the time. All I can remember about when I arrived is that there seemed to be a huge amount of stairs. In reality there were only about ten but I was so small that just getting into the place felt like it took an age. The anticipation was building!

I walked into what seemed to be an exaggerated social club with lounge sofas and a bar that sold crisps and cans of pop. Behind the bar was Iris. She was expecting us, and she greeted my mum by name. As I looked about the room I saw it was decorated in tinsel, neon lights, fairy lights and trophies of all sizes, gold and silver, all on display. We were then led down some more stairs to the disco floor, which had even more neon lights, a big old disco ball spinning on the ceiling and a dance floor that was so shiny you could do you hair in it. The room was filled with girls between the ages of 5 and 15 all spinning, leaping, kicking, and shrieking about, and to my dismay there was not a boy in sight. The place was full of energy and for a three year old it was very overwhelming. I grabbed a tighter hold of my mum's hand.

Behind the DJ booth was Iris's son Derek, who'd seen us arrive and came over to meet us. Looking back at it now, he would have reminded me of George Michael - he was the spit. He spoke to my mum. "Hi Val, so this Raymond," he said looking down at me.

"Yes, this is Raymond," my Mum replied. "He is always entertaining and really wants to learn to dance, don't you, Son!"

At this point I came over really shy. I don't know if it

was the lights, the noise, the girls or that I was just in such a bizarre place. I hid behind my mum's legs and all I could think about was getting out of that place. To this day, my mum cannot believe how I acted the first time I met Derek. Derek took my hand. "Come on Raymond, come with me and I'll introduce you to the girls."

"Go on Raymond!" my mum encouraged me, but I wouldn't let her out of my sight, so she came onto the middle of the dance floor with Derek and me as the music died down. Derek motioned to the dance floor. "Hi, Girls! I'd like you to meet Raymond. Do you think we can make him welcome?" It seemed like in unison all the girls turned and said, "Hi Raymond!" I remember feeling like I just wanted to get out of this place. I was wearing my Adidas tracksuit that my mum, who happened to be a seamstress, had amazingly turned into a Lacoste tracksuit by sowing on a Lacoste crocodile logo.

To start with I hated my visits to those disco classes! The first time I sat there and just cried cos there were too many girls and I was very embarrassed; I didn't get up at all, just sat there watching. The second time was a bit better and I got up and did my first 'up out kick'. I followed the line of girls, with one other boy named Ian who appeared on the second week and made me feel better being there with all those girls. He was about ten and I remember watching him in awe, as he could spin, jump up in the air and end up in the splits. I remember looking on and thinking to myself, I want to be that good and I want to be better. The whole room was watching and cheering him on. Derek asked me if I wanted to be like that and I told him yes, so Derek told me to go with Ian and he would help me. With dancing, you first have to learn to dance solo. After about six weeks I did my first competition that way, and I absolutely loved it, I came home with a massive trophy, and even though I'd only competed against six other boys, I was so proud of myself. Dancing was not as popular for boys back then - not like it is now, especially not up in Liverpool. My mum never forced me to go to lessons; if I didn't want to go I didn't have to, but I enjoyed them so much that I would ask her to take me and couldn't wait to get there. She would always ask me if I was sure, but off I would always go. I loved it.

When I was about five Mum was finding it difficult to drive me to and from Bootle, so she looked for a place a little closer and found the Chiltern Castings in West Derby. They taught every sort of dance there and at the time my mum thought it would be good for me to learn all the different forms if I really wanted to make a living out of it. I did manage to convince her to keep taking me to Millington's to carry on the disco dancing though. Derek knew I was going to be good and was always complimentary and supportive. He told my mum I was a 'phenomenon'. I didn't know what he meant - didn't understand the word - and I don't think my mum did either because when I asked her, she said, "I don't know Son, but best you keep doing what you're doing as Derek seems very happy with you. My mum was happy, my teacher was happy, so I was happy too. Derrick partnered me up with Natalie Wilcox when I was seven. She was unbelievable for a seven year old!

We were soon on the local ITV News and within six months we had won every competition we entered. We were that 'phenomenon' that Derek had spotted. Natalie was so tiny and so graceful, like a feather going through the air - she was amazing. The only trouble was that when we went away for competitions she would get home-sick and want to be back with her mum. I felt sorry for her at the time.

At the same time I had also become British Champion for Disco Dancing Solo and Natalie and I were Rock 'n' Roll champions. I was kept very busy.

As my dad was away most of the time working and my mum was working full time on the market, the school summer holidays were a slight problem. Mum was very protective of me; she didn't like me playing out on the street and when I did play out I was only allowed around the corner. Then one summer when I was nine she saw an advert in the local Echo, and I was taken along to 'Chiltern Castings Summer School,' which was £80 a week. Chiltern Castings was based in another part of Liverpool and used this place in the summer. It was a lot of money in those days but my mum saw it as a good way to keep me safely off the street. It was a typical theatrical dance school with pictures of ballet dancers on the wall and posters of musicals all over the place, and it was owned by a lady called Mrs. Byatt. She was very old school 1950's glam, blonde and always wore a fur coat. Very classy and theatrical, she was a lovely lady and as time went on she mothered me.

The place was once again full of girls and there was a lady there called Miss Suzanne. She was lovely too and she sat with me when I first arrived. I kept looking round to make sure my mum was still there and hadn't left me, but I must've soon forgotten all about her because unbeknown to me she sneaked out the back of the class after being given the nod to leave from Miss Suzanne. To this day I can't remember Miss Suzanne's surname - we just always called her 'Miss Suzanne' and that's how I will always fondly remember her.

I ended up that day loving this class and when my mum came to collect me at four o'clock I couldn't wait to bound over the rise in the car park to tell her how fab it was and what I had been doing. "It was such good fun, Mum! Can I go back tomorrow?" It must have been music to Mum's ears. "Sound!" she said and smiled. This was two birds with one stone: I was enjoying myself *and* I was getting kept off the streets and was somewhere safe while she was working. This summer school was fantastic. I learnt drama as well as singing and all new different types of dance. A film I was really keen on at the time was 'Singing in the Rain'. I remember sitting down one Sunday afternoon and watching this with my mum and I just loved it. The energy, the dance moves blew me away; it was just so cool and slick how Gene Kelly would move with effortless efficiency.

The drama and singing was all new to me and I loved every minute of it, but I was still doing disco with Natalie at Derek's. Mrs Byatt wanted me primarily at her school but I wanted to do both, so on Tuesday and Saturday mornings I went to Mrs Byatt's drama and singing lessons and on a Tuesday and Saturday afternoon I went to Derek's dance school. The teachers were very territorial and wanted me solely to themselves. Looking back now I realise my poor mum must have been exhausted running me round to each lesson as well as going to work, but I was only a kid. That's what mums do!

My dad was working away a lot at this time and didn't manage to come to see any of my competitions: not because he didn't want to, he just couldn't. I remember he came to one competition and stood at the side on his own watching me in disbelief and with tears in his eyes. As I stepped off the dance floor after my heat he was rubbing his eyes quick, so not to let me see his emotion. "What do you think of me dancing, Dad?" I asked, skipping towards him so pleased to see him there. He told me he hadn't realised how good I was, how proud he was of what I had achieved and how sad that he'd missed out on so much of what I'd already done because of his work. At that moment I think he realised this was going to be more than a hobby. This was what I was going to be doing for the rest of my life.

***

By now my teacher Mrs Byatt had started to see potential in me and was giving my dance lessons at nearly half price to help my mum out a bit. A few stars had already passed through Mrs Byatt's hands and she also acted as an agent, so I guess she was keen to keep me. It was Mrs Byatt who had spotted Jennifer Ellison and unbeknown to me she was a casting agent for the local soap 'Brookside'. Funnily enough, the one class I hated at Mrs Byatt's School was Mrs Headspeath's: it was a lot of reading and repeating and I hated it, but as it happens it was her class that stood me in good stead for the future.

Natalie's mum Cal wanted her to specialise in ballroom, tap, single and disco. Natalie's parents were better off than mine. They came from an affluent area, lived in a big house with a studio in it and they could afford all the expensive dance lessons, shoes and costumes that went with it, which mine unfortunately couldn't. There were not enough hours in the day for my mum to fit in two jobs and all the classes, and as I was so young and was unable to make my mind up what I wanted to do my mum had to make some of those decisions for me. Mum and Dad also wanted me to quit Mrs Byatt's, which I didn't want because I loved it there. I had already given up the disco dancing, as we could not afford to do both. Now the costs were building up - £18 a lesson here, £25 a lesson there, plus the costumes and the running around. I was lucky I had a mum like I did, otherwise none of the things that came later would ever have happened. A decision had to be made, so I parted company with Natalie, although we stayed firm friends, and Bryony became my new dance partner.

***

It's a tough old game in the dancing world even at the age of ten - a dog eat dog world where everyone's after the best they can get. There were pushy mums everywhere wanting their kids to be up the front, and there was a lot of politics involving who was to dance with who, who taught who. My mum was approached by the parents of some of the best dancers on the circuit wanting their daughters to partner me. I was so small, though, that most of them were too tall. I was the runt of the Quinn litter - even my dad's nick name for me was Titch! This was when Bryony became my partner. At this time I also auditioned with Elsie Kelly for a Lost Boy part in the pantomime production of Peter Pan, with Unis from Gladiators, (then a popular prime-time TV show) as the headliner. It wore me out, as it was 7-8 weeks over Christmas, but it was my very first paid job and I was going to earn the grand sum of £1.50 a show. I guess children didn't really get paid in those days; even the mums didn't get paid for being chaperones. It was considered more of an opportunity for kids to take a step in the right direction if they wanted to get into the business.

The show was a great experience and so much fun. I was no longer practising - this was the real deal. I remember on the opening night I was so excited and nervous having lines to say! I found it a bit weird when the chaperones were putting our make up on, only to be told 'that's show biz', but to this day I still try not to wear make-up. While we were waiting for the show to start I could hear the noise of the auditorium filling. The tannoy announced 'This is your Act One Beginners', the curtain went up and the show began. As my scene was about to start I remember my heart racing and I couldn't speak to anyone because I had to stay focused on putting heart and soul into my part. I only had eight lines, but I was leader of the Lost Boys and felt under so much pressure. Soon as I entered centre stage the buzz was incredible and I was hooked: there was no going back now.

I remember being on stage with all those people in the theatre looking at me; I remember looking down at the seat four rows back to see a young child sitting where I'd once sat with my mum. I was now that boy I had told my mum I wanted to be.

Chapter 2

Brookside Years

At the age of ten I got my first acting part in a British soap called 'Brookside' after secretly going to the audition with only Mrs Byatt and my mum knowing. The show was broadcast on Channel 4 three nights a week at eight o'clock and had already been running for twenty one years. It was the brain child of Phil Redmond the writer of Grange Hill and had regular viewing figures of over a million at its peak. Everybody loved Brookside! It was the first real 'scouse' show – it *felt* real, and to be honest if it hadn't ended I would probably still be there. Mrs Byatt set up the audition, which was held in an office on the set of Brookside in Childwall, home of what was then Mersey TV. Phil Redmond had wanted realism in his show, so he'd created a breakthrough concept by buying a total of thirteen houses in a real Liverpool street; six were used on screen and the remaining seven for post-production, admin and welfare. After the show got cancelled, the houses were sold back to the public and the street is still there with people living their normal lives.

There was a role up for grabs for a boy aged about ten years old and there were about sixty other lads at the auditions. We all had our photographs individually taken and we were dwindled down and down. The main aspect of the part was that you were joining a family, so the initial requirement was that you had to look a bit like Bernie Nolan and Neil Caple, who played the parents of the character. They had already cast the brother and sister roles.

The casting was done in a tiny little room at Mersey TV, now known as Lime Pictures. Dorothy Andrews was the casting director and she was with another girl, Joanna Aicher. They kept cutting and whittling the group down, and then I was given two pages of script to learn by the end of the day. I had ten scenes and I had never done anything like this before, but I knew I wanted to be on TV and this was my chance. Those lessons that I hated with Miss Headspeath had now paid off, as the script reading came easy to me. Thanks to her, digesting lines was not an issue, and learning them off by heart definitely helped me to focus.

Eventually we were whittled down to just two. (I knew the other lad from Chiltern Castings; he was called James we were not friends as such, but had seen each other knocking about and he had lighter hair than myself. James later went on to star in Joseph and the 'Amazing Technicolor Dream Coat'. That evening we were sent home and told we would hear from the studio in the next few days as to who had been selected.

The next day was like any other day for me, just a normal one at school. When I got home that evening my mum acted like normal and then she said matter of factly. "Guess what, Son, you got it. You got the part!"

"Shut up!" was the only thing I could think of to say. Even now, writing about it gives me goose bumps. This was a massive step for me - Brookside was massive - and I was a very happy little boy.

The strange thing was that the night before the audition my mum had taken me to see 'Blood Brothers' on stage at the Liverpool Empire, starring the very 'Bernie Nolan' I was about to start to work with. The theatre was full and the only seats we could get had restricted view, but that didn't bother me, I loved it. Little did I know then that I was going to be working with Bernie and she would be the one playing my on-screen mother, Diane Murray. 'Blood Brothers' had me in tears that night. I was a bit of a 'queen' in those younger years!

Later on, when we first met Bernie on the set of 'Brookside' my mum told her "We watched you on stage the other night in 'Blood Brothers."

Bernie replied, "Oh I, you should've rung me! You could have come back stage."

"Well, we couldn't ring you, because we didn't know you!" my mum said.

It was funny at the time.

Bernie had an amazing presence about her. I remember being on set with her for the first time and everyone there having this nervous energy because she was 'Bernie Nolan' from the 'Nolans'. Neil Caple and I were stood outside the house in the Close and Bernie was doing a scene through the front window. We heard the director scream, 'Action!' and Bernie slowly walked towards the window taking a longing look out to the other side of the street. I turned to Neil and said, "I can't believe Bernie Nolan is playing my mum."

He smiled down at me. "Your mum? She's playing my wife: I get to kiss her!"

I joined the show in early 2000 and played the character Anthony Murray. I was a member of a new family that was coming to live in the Close and I appeared in the show until in finished in 2003. My first day filming was not on the Brookside set, as we were first filmed as a family packing up the house ready to move to our new home on 'the Close'. I remember I had no lines - I had to hide in the attic, as my character didn't want to move house. It was supposed to be an old house, very dusty and with cobwebs everywhere, and because I had to be in the loft there was no light up there and I was left at certain points with the trap door closed in the pitch black. But I wasn't scared. (Not!)

It was amazing being on set and being one of the actors. I could eat what I wanted, I had a Winnebago, and I didn't have to pay for anything: it was so different to what I was used to. There was a runner on set and they would ask me what I wanted and the runner would go and get it for me. Because I was only a minor I had to be looked after and a lady called Sue Taylor was my chaperone. Sue became like my step mom, and I loved her - she still comes to everything I do now. I loved being fussed over, and like my mum she used to tickle my back or my arm. This was something my mum had done to me for years and my nan, God bless her, used to do it for hours. It's my little weak spot, and nothing has changed!

After the first shoot it took about four weeks for the episode to appear on television. I remember the night it was shown on Channel 4 everyone came round ours to watch the episode on TV. Mum and I had already seen it, as Channel 4 had given us a private screening at the studio in Liverpool. It was all very exciting and our lounge was buzzing. Everyone was there – nan, my brothers, uncles, aunties, Mum and Dad and the dog's cousin!! This was an event. My mum recorded it on video tape, and she still has the tape to this day. When the show finished she rewound it and we watched it all over again. I think we watched it three times and the family clapped and cheered every time. When I was told to go to bed and my dad had gone to the pub and everyone had left I could hear through the walls my mum watching the episode again with a glass of wine. That's mothers for you!

There was media build up on telly, but I hadn't told any of my school mates. No one even knew I danced. When I went to school after the first show was aired the headmaster said, "I've seen you on Brookside, Raymond. Very good!" The kids at school weren't really bothered as I didn't have that many close friends at school. Those that said anything were generally taking the piss, but that's kids for ya. Kids I was friends with lived round the corner from Mum's house; they were the kids I hung about with. I was never at school long enough to form firm friendships, I was sort of a loner at school. The truth is I was in one day out the next and I had a lot of time off with no further education beyond that. In those days they didn't have a tutor on set. I had no real interest in school anyway, but with all my time away I was becoming less and less interested. I didn't mind lessons like art and graphics. They were my best subjects because they grabbed my imagination, held my attention and tested my creativity. PE wasn't really my thing, especially not football, which was too aggressive for me. I was small for my age and not one for rough and tumble. While I was starting out in Brookside I was still going to Mrs Byatt's dance school. After filming I had a certain amount of time to learn script, then go to ballroom, then practice, then have my tea. My day was literally full to the brim and I guess my schooling did suffer. Learning the script wasn't that bad; the older actors in the show were allowed to ad-lib a little, but I didn't. I did everything I was told, I didn't want to mess up my chances.

One day a new director turned up on the Brookside set. He was really handsome like George Clooney, but he was also very strict and wanted the scripts word for word. This upset some of the actors, as they had been ad-libbing their scripts for a few years now, and there were some clashes between him and the cast, but it was all above my head. What did happen round about now, though, was I got a bit comfortable on set - started to mess about a bit, got a bit cocky - and I remember to this day when Neil Caple, who played Marty Murray, took me to one side and had a firm word with me.

"I know this is fun and you're a young man, and you have a long road in front of you I'm sure of it. Just a little piece of advice: it's all about how you conduct yourself on set; you need to be professional and treat people with respect. Don't lose your head and don't lose who you are." He put his hand on my shoulder. "You're a wonderfully talented young man with a bright future ahead of you, so I'm telling you this now to help you keep focused on your future goals. You need to concentrate on the job in hand, Raymond, and not get distracted from what you are employed to do. You're only as good as your reputation, so stay professional at all times."

I think it was the best bit of advice I could have had at such a tender age, and from that day on I have taken everything I do seriously. It's such a competitive world the entertainment business, where everyone knows everyone, and you do not want to get a bad name as it closes all the doors for you in the future.

The writers changed and the producers changed. They were all trying to do things different ways and the show was struggling to maintain its position. By late November 2002 the show had been transferred to what was known as 'the graveyard slot', four-thirty to six on a Saturday afternoon. The cast was reduced and we were now filming for a ninety minute show. Things were changing on set but again this was all above me; I didn't know anything about the commercial side of TV, but I did know it could be very hard work - sometimes I would have to shoot fourteen scenes in a day. We'd get the main bulk of the show done, and then the sub scenes would be filmed, sometimes late at night to get night shots, and even up to one in the morning. For me at my age staying up late was great but tiring; it was all an adventure and very exciting.

I was still very much into my dancing whilst acting in Brookside, and in March 2000 I entered the British Open along with my partner Bryony. It was being held at the World Tower Ballroom in Blackpool, with dancers coming from all over the world. It was a really big thing. My mum thought maybe telling Bryony's parents that I was in Brookside would lead them to think it would affect my dancing. They wanted us to be professional dancers and that was all - but we won, so she didn't have to worry after all! A family holiday was planned in order for everyone to recoup after all the hard work we'd been doing, and we went to Italy in the June of that same year, but Bryony didn't want to enter the Italian dance competitions so she didn't come. Me and my mum just watched the dancing, enjoyed the sunshine and had a lovely time for the first week, then Dad came out for the second week. It was fantastic!

Anyway, when we came back from Italy Bryony and I split up our dance partnership because I guess I wasn't really focusing on the dancing because of my commitment to Brookside. Stacey Parrott from Bournemouth, chosen by Margaret Redmond, was to be my new partner. Margaret was the best teacher there was, so Stacey used to travel for five hours to dance with me! She was a little, delicate girl; most girls were too tall for me back then, as I was so small myself, and they also wore little heels that made me look even smaller. When Stacey and I started having lessons, she would stay with us at weekends, but it all got too much for her and my mum. We were entered into a competition at the Winter Gardens which fell on the same day that I had scenes to do at Brookside. We didn't tell Stacey, but I had a scene at five pm for Brookside, and the final for the Winter Gardens if we got through would be eight pm.

"What we going to do?" I said to my mum.

"Don't worry, Son, I'll sort it out!"

Mum, Dad and I got in the car that afternoon and did a

dummy run from Blackpool to Liverpool to make sure they knew exactly how long it took, "Don't park - I'll jump out, you pick us up!" For Dancing you have exact times for each dance, so we knew the exact time we had to be back. We had two hours and fifteen minutes to get to the Brookside set and back again, but it was a simple scene, just me getting filmed walking down the alleyway. We left Stacey and her mum without telling them where we'd gone, and I thought it was all very funny and exciting at the time. We made it, though! I did the Brookside scene, then jumped into the car and got changed back into my dance outfit while my mum was driving along - which may sound easier than it was, as there are so many bits to a tail suit. Besides the cufflinks, each individual button has a tiny little screw, and there are loads down the front of the jacket; the whole thing is fitted together piece by piece, so it was really hard to put on at the best of times, let alone in the back seat of the car as it was weaving around the roads trying to get back in time to compete in the dance competition final.

Just as we got back to the hall they called my number and I was like, "Dad! Help me quick!" as I was running in still doing up screws on my jacket.

"Where have you been?" Stacey asked in a panicked voice.

"Oh, just out for lunch. We on?" I asked her in a blasé manner, still a bit panicky myself from trying to do my screw buttons up.

It was the weirdest day ever. Amazingly enough we came fifth, but it was getting to be very hard work for Stacey what with all the travelling, so inevitably we didn't last long and Stacey and I went our separate ways.

Talking of funny stories, there's one about my mum, my nan and me when we had to stay in a hotel in Blackpool. It was at the height of the Easter season, with dancers everywhere and kids on their school holidays. Blackpool was buzzing and packed and all the hotels and B&Bs were fully booked. We had been dancing all day and so mum decided that we should stay overnight, which was easier said than done. We couldn't believe our luck when we managed to find a room - £70 it was. We were so tired we could have slept in a bus shelter, which in all honesty we should have done because when we got into the room it was filthy. The sheets were stained, the wardrobe door was hanging off and the room stunk of I don't know what, but if it was a colour it would be brown! My mum put my poor nan on top of the bed covers in a sleeping bag with her coat on.

A couple of hours later Mum said, "Ray are you awake? Get up, Mother!" It was four o'clock in the morning.

"Mum, I can't sleep!"

"I know, Son. Get ya coat on!"

Nan was up, we were all up. The place was the pits, and we left.

It wasn't funny at the time, but looking back it makes me smile and it still makes my mum laugh. The good old days, eh!

***

Of course, with Stacey gone I had no dance partner at all, but we still went on the circuit. Pontin's was the next stop on the itinerary; all my dance friends were there and we would stay the weekend, so off we went. If I'm honest it was more for my mum than me - the circuit had become her social life - so even though I wasn't dancing there we were, and I'd watch and learn from what everyone else was up to, what they were doing.

That was when I first saw a girl called Kirsty. She was dancing with someone else at that time, but I thought she was a decent dancer and could see potential if she had the right teacher.

"She would be alright for you, Raymond," my mum said, and I watched her dance. She was the right height and had a lot of energy in her movements.

Kirsty turned out to be older than me by a year. I was 13 and had just started dancing as a Junior Section; Kirsty was already dancing Junior. After a while of dancing together we formed a close friendship. We were good together as dancers and made a mark on the circuit and the dance floor, but we struggled to achieve the consistency I'd had with Bryony. On the other hand, Juniors was a higher level and there were a lot more dancers to compete with.

Being an actor the same time as I was at school certainly made life interesting. I went to Rudston Junior as a child, and have fond memories of that school. As a teenager I went to Gateacre Comprehensive, which isn't used as a school any more. It was an old building and I remember it being always cold. It was tinny and falling apart, and the place was full of graffiti, some of which I had a hand in. As you can imagine, being in a local soap opera and being treated differently from my school mates made me a target for a bit of banter.

I was let off homework because of my work-load filming, and I was a favourite of a couple of the dinner ladies, our Madge and Babs. I think they had a soft spot for me because I loved my food!

The banter was what every school kid goes through, and if you stick out from the crowd you are going to be more of a target. At one point it was reported in the press that I was bullied at school. This I can tell you is misleading: if any sort of name-calling is bullying, then every kid that ever went to school has been bullied. I would be called names, get into fights, run away from fights, and when needed play the cocky, arrogant dick. I could handle myself. To be fair, *I* wouldn't like you if I knew you were getting let off from doing your homework!

One of my mates at school was Karl Pilkinson, who's now a bouncer on the doors I think, in Liverpool. His dad had a motorbike that I used to go on the back of every now and then, unbeknown to my parents, which I didn't mind because it was 'cool'. Mostly, though, I didn't fit in at school, and looking back now that was not necessarily a bad thing. When you grow up you realise it's not always best to follow the crowd. The Sun newspaper later on wrote an article about me headed 'Bullied - Look At Me Now!' but they took things I said and twisted them. It seemed to be a local pastime for lads hanging around the streets to egg my mum and dad's house. My dad even painted it canary yellow because it got egged so many times. I remember way back whilst I was filming in Brookside I had to have my head shaved for a plot line, but the lads at school thought it was sound and I was accepted as 'one of them' for a change, so I went along with it. One guy came up to me and said, "Is right Lad, you're one of us now!" and ruffled my number 1 haircut.

They were all listening to heavy rap music in those days and still are. Back then 50 Cents and G Unit were the craze, and we used to wear G Unit trainers in black so the teacher thought they were school shoes. I loved my hair, though - I've got good hair and I hope I keep it, so when I had to shave it off it was a bit embarrassing. The other kids loved it though, so I was happy with that for a while.

***

Brookside was such a massive show to me and a lot of others around me, especially my nan, God rest her. She was a big fan. I was so young at first, but after a while it began to feel normal. I was going to the same place every day, with the same people, and I used to really look forward to it. Being on set with all the adults, I learnt very quickly to deal with certain situations like an adult: I had to grow up very fast. Even though I was so young, I desperately wanted to fit in, to be part of the team and not seen as just the little child actor. I wanted to be taken seriously and I was really eager to impress. They used to swear a lot and there was a lot of banter but luckily I was used to that growing up around my dad and my brothers! My Mum was worried that I always seemed to have a lot to learn, but Bernie Nolan told her, "Don't worry Val, trust me! After a few weeks it'll become second nature", and it did. I was like a little sponge, soaking it all up and learning everything and each day it got easier.

Over time the story-line began to get difficult for me, as the character I played started to go through some very hard times. There was one particular scene I'll never forget because they needed me to cry on-screen. For quite a while I'd been putting myself in situations that made me feel down; the build up to this particular scene took months and it really began to get to me. I started not going out as much and spent a lot of time on my own, wrapped up in my own thoughts. I didn't really notice at the time but as I look back now, the acting I was doing was affecting me. There were days I would go on set knowing a certain scene was happening and I would start thinking and being a certain way beforehand, so that when I got to the scene itself there was a build-up of emotions inside of me that would then burst out on camera. What made it more difficult was if we had to shoot the scene again. A re-take could be for anything, not necessarily the actors getting it wrong; it could be a bad camera angle, or because a camera lens had gone soft or a sound man had picked up a stray sound such a car horn or an aircraft.

Eventually the day came for the climax of the storyline. I remember leaving school early and going to Reception to sign in with my teacher, and then half an hour later when everyone else was going to their first class I was picked up to go to the studio. When I arrived I sat in the Green Room with a Crunchy and a cup of tea and Neil Caple came in to see me.

He sat down next to me and asked if I was OK. "Yep!" I said, to which he replied. "I only ask because I know this is a big day for you." He looked concerned. "There are a lot of big scenes for you in the schedule today. I just want to make sure you're in the right head space, as there's one scene in particular that if you do it right could stand you in good stead for the future."

By this time I had already zoned out into the character I was about to play, and I really wasn't thinking about it any more. I knew my lines, I knew I had to cry. I was ready to do it, and now I just wanted to get it over with. I certainly hadn't put much thought into what impact this scene would have on me and the watching public and what Neil said took me by surprise. If anything though, it made me more determined to do it right, as I'd always looked up to him and I didn't want to let him down.

As the day went on, it was like I was doing all my scenes back to back in a structured way, so by default the last one was bound to be the scene Neil had spoken to me about, the crux of the story line. If I'm honest, that scene had been on my mind and staring at me from the schedule listed on the notice board all day, and as the hours went by I was all too well aware that it was getting closer. By the time the scene was to be shot Neil had left for the day, but I had his words in my head encouraging me to get it right. I remember going over to the director when everything was in place and asking him, "Do you think this scene can be done in one take?"

He looked at me and said, "Well yes, it can be if you get it right!" and laughed in a blasé way. It was just another day on set for him but I had it in my head that I only wanted to do this scene once, so I went for it – determined there'd be no way they'd think they could get a better performance out of me. It had been a long day; it was now cold and dark outside and after a long camera rehearsal it was time to record.

In this particular scene I was being dragged out of my house by my school bully's family. They were looking for their daughter and knew that I had information about her whereabouts. Before we started I had said to the lad that played my bully's brother, "Do what you would if this was real, and don't be scared of hurting me," to which he had readily agreed. I didn't really know the lad as I'd only ever shot one or two scenes with him, but I knew the type of performance I was about to give and I wanted to back it up with realism.

"Lights, Camera, and…..Action!" was screamed across set by the director.

To my relief the scene was shot in one take to huge applause from cast and crew. "Was that good?" I just spoke out to no one in particular, then looking around I saw that Bernie Nolan had tears in her eyes. My heart was in my stomach when the director asked, "Did you get it?" To my relief the scene was in the can and that was it, over!

That was the scene I was nominated for at the British Soap Awards in 2002 for Best Dramatic Performance. The Awards were held at the BBC's White City studios; I went up to London with my mum and everyone from the cast was at the event. I was thirteen at the time, but still only looked about ten! I was given a seat number and sat in the auditorium. The show seemed to last for ever and I remember being a bag of nervous energy waiting for my category to come up. It was one of the last of the night and when at last it did come up I was thinking to myself, 'Oh, oh! Here we go!' My mum nudged my leg all excited for me, which got me even worse for the nerves. I was up against five other scenes, from East Enders, Emmerdale, Crossroads, Doctors, Holly Oaks and Coronation Street. Mine was fourth one in, and after they'd all been shown there was no real pause before Ben Elton called my name out as the winner. I couldn't believe it! Of course, I had to go up on stage and do an acceptance speech, and this had caught me by surprise as I really didn't expect to win. Everyone had told me to get a speech ready but I hadn't: to my way of thinking, if I was putting a speech together it would mean I was expecting to win and I wasn't!

Standing on the stage on my own with tears streaming from my eyes, I thanked everyone who had helped me get there with this award in my hand. I was surprised I had to walk backstage afterwards for press interviews. Someone told me that if I gave them the award, they would box it and give it back to me when I left at the end of the night. I reluctantly handed it over. I got back to my seat eventually and was surprised that there were camera crews about after the show had finished asking us to clap and laugh so they could use these scenes when editing the programme before it went out on air. Later on there was an after-show party, which I went to with my mum, and from what I can remember everyone got quite drunk. It was on this occasion that I had a picture taken with Louis Walsh.

***

My time with Brookside lasted three years. Eighteen months before the show was cancelled by Channel 4 the producer at Mersey Television called the cast into a meeting to break the news. The older actors had seen it coming but I was oblivious. I was only fourteen, and was just having the time of my life. I remember at the time feeling a bit gutted; this programme was part of my life and this was my job. It suddenly dawned on me that I was about to lose my job and lose my income. This was the end of an era for me and it was going to change my life completely. The actors on set all took it in different ways: some were sad, some nervous and some seemed to be relieved it was over. I was very young at the time and didn't really understand what it was all about; as far as I was concerned the show being cancelled came out of the blue. I remember there being a big meeting with Phil Redmond and he explained that although Channel 4 had cancelled the show, Channel 5, a new TV channel that had just started broadcasting on British TV were interested and Phil wanted to go out with a bang and get some really good writers on it. The older actors had had a feeling that something was going on because they said the scripts hadn't been as good lately.

The other actors always treated me well. My particular favourites were Illy he was a director a scouser a really nice guy everyone loved him, and Cathy from the Canteen who knew exactly how I liked my eggs and save me the hash browns, and we still speak to each other now. It was a real Liverpool clique with everyone knowing each other, and I even ended up buying a house opposite one of them. To this day when any of us meet it's great, like no time has passed at all.

Brookside paid per episode and there was no special

children's contract, I received the same amount for each episode. All my money went into a bank account that my mum had organised for me; half went into a savings account and half towards my dancing and acting costs, plus I was allowed a little pocket money for my phone and bits and pieces. One day soon after the show finished I sat down with my mum and she showed me a bank account with £40,000 in it, and I remember saying, "Cor, Mum, we got all that! God, Mum we're rich!" This was the money I had earned on the show and that my mum had looked after for me. It was enough to buy a house – and that was what she did!

It was announced by Channel 4 on the 11th June, 2003 that the final show would be aired in November of that year. The last Brookside - divided into three distinct parts - was televised on Channel 4 at 22:40 on 4th November, two days after the 21st anniversary of the show. It went out to an audience of 2.27 Million. The story line for the final show was my family leaving the very Close we had entered five years before. My on-screen mum Bernie had already left the show and the rest of us were leaving to start another new life. I had really enjoyed my time there and I didn't want it to end. I am a very emotional person even now, and I remember getting quite upset. I was given a posh glass paperweight with my name on and the start and finish date of my time in Brookside. Oh, and a key ring which - yes! - I still have. My mum keeps everything I win, souvenirs of everything I do or star in; every script, every certificate, trophy, picture and magazine. There was a wrap party when the show finished, but I did not attend. This was the end of Brookside and my first insight into life as an unemployed actor looking for work.

At the time the show finished I had just a few months left before my exams. The only one I passed was art, which was a subject I enjoyed and another way for me to express myself. I still have my finest piece of art. I had to sum up myself in one picture - Nat West bank account, Buzz Lightyear, Fanta Can, and Everton Shirt and a skateboard wheel!

**

It wasn't long before I started getting really frustrated: nothing was happening, nothing was on the cards. I was expecting an influx of offers now that Brookside had finished and I got nothing. Life as a known actor is not as easy as some people would imagine; it's a hard and competitive world. Then eventually after much time waiting I was approached to do Mersey Beat. I only did one episode, playing a troubled child called Leon Marsh.

After Mersey Beat my next job was 'Singing Cactus', a BBC afternoon drama, I played the character John Reilly alongside the great Melanie Hill, best known for 'Bread', and the amazing Peter Capaldi. Melanie became a big part of my life, and from when I was 16, every time I went to London I would stay with her. I would go for weekends with my mum and Melanie Hill would pick us up. First time I ever saw her house I thought, 'God, she's minted!' It was a beautiful old Victorian cottage, very big and in the middle of Muswell Hill by the tube station.

Next came A to Z, which I was told was going to be massive, a young British version of Friends. I filmed five episodes, but these episodes never came to light even though the budget was big. One day the TV channel just dropped it. I was starting to learn that the business I was in was not an easy, straightforward one. Everything had started coming to a standstill on the acting side and I suddenly realised that I couldn't rely on just the one avenue, so I decided to explore the others I had left behind. I started focusing more on singing, with Miss Suzanne who was giving private lessons at our house. I carved my name into her piano when I was bored one day, though why I thought I could get away with it I don't know. Yeah, its got Ray Q on it – it's still there to this day!

I couldn't sing for toffee at the time, even though the whole point of Mrs Byatt's School was that everyone should sing, dance and act. It was a drama school and everyone was aspiring to be somebody in the entertainment world. As I got better at singing, though, my confidence grew. At the age of about fifteen, a typical teenager who thought he knew everything, I was placed in a boy band with some lads from the dance school and this band was pencilled in to be called 'Eaton Road'. At the time boy bands were in vogue, and Mrs Byatt had been approached by a record label to put one together. The other lads selected were Daniel Morris, James Edwards, David Heath and Anthony Hannah. We were asked to go to a meeting with Mrs Byatt to discuss the project, but my heart wasn't in it. I didn't want be in a boy band, I wanted to do my own thing. She asked us to come back on the following Wednesday dressed as a boy band so that we could be filmed doing some numbers for the record company, to see what they had to say. I didn't do any research - just turned up in my usual clothes. I wasn't really interested and knew what my decision was going to be, regardless. I didn't ask any questions about the record label or anything else: I was totally uninterested. I only went along for the experience.

Before the Wednesday we had some practice sessions at the school with Mrs Byatt and her daughter Michelle, who was the dance teacher. The other lads were well into it and saw it as a big opportunity but I felt like I was wasting their time. I did make my views clear to Mrs Byatt right from the outset, but not to the lads. When the day came we were dressed up like a schoolboy version of 'Steps' and we performed the harmonies and dance moves we were told to. I dutifully went through the motions of performing and Mrs Byatt and Michelle were happy with what we got on film. Mrs Byatt said, "I'm sure they're going to like that. I can't say how long it'll be until they get back to us, but well done for your efforts!"

As far as I was concerned, that was me done with being in a boy band and when the other lads had left I asked Mrs Byatt if we could have a quick chat in her office. I told her then that this was not for me and that I really didn't want to be in a boy band, but I couldn't tell the lads to their faces. I put it to her that I would be very grateful if she could have a word with them to explain where I was coming from, and to my relief she was very understanding about it.

Chapter 3

Post Brookside

After so many lessons with Miss Suzanne I felt more relaxed about singing in public and I started singing in pubs around Liverpool that were owned by friends of the family. These were good nights that were a lot of fun, and it was working in places like social clubs on Bingo Nights. My confidence increased and I was beginning to find my feet as a performer. This is when my love of swing started. My dad used to play off what he called his 'wireless' and every now and again you would hear him shout up to my mum from the bottom of the stairs, "Val, where's my wireless?" He used to play classic swing music - all the golden oldies and the Top Hundred Hits. One day I heard a song I particularly liked, 'My Special Angel' by Malcolm Vaughan, and I went into the back room where Dad was cleaning the eight foot fish tank that he had made himself and asked him what it was. "The best music you'll ever hear in your life, Son!" From that moment I was hooked on swing and it was a natural transition for me when I was performing myself to aspire to be like the artists that had inspired me. From then on the songs I would be practising with Miss Suzanne were the songs my dad would listen to.

The more gigs I did the more confident I became. I didn't get much advice from other performers apart from watching artists that were current on TV at the time. I used to watch videos nearly every night while I did my homework! I knew the most important thing I had to learn was how to be a crown pleasing performer. My mum always understood that, and would get me to sit down and watch certain films, like Singing in the Rain with Gene Kelly, and study how they performed. My life so far had been led by competition so competing in something to do with singing seemed to be the natural next step.

The first big gig I secured was when the Tsunami hit Thailand and an event was set up in Liverpool to help raise funds for the survivors. It was a Neville Skelly fund raiser in the Philharmonic Theatre, a Big Band affair. The experience of a big audience was going to be great experience for me, but it wasn't a normal audition. My mum's sister, our Sue worked at Barnardo's, which was connected to the show. Via the back door, shall we say, we got call from Neville Skelly himself, (he was a big thing in Liverpool at the time) saying, "Yes, I think we can get Ray to do one song." It was unbelievable for me! My mum took me out to get a nice suit from M&S and she stuck diamonds on my tie, which made me feel very show biz, and added a lot to my confidence. I felt good and I looked good; it was a brilliant success and I loved every minute of it. Standing in front of a big crowd like that was my first taster of what the future could be like for me. I did one song, before I went on, I was so nervous. Then when I stepped on stage I can remember feeling slightly out of control, bouncing around like a Duracell bunny. When I left the stage I was so hyped with nervous energy I bounced around the back stage as well! My mum and dad were ecstatic, and thoroughly enjoyed my performance. If there's one thing I don't take for granted it's the opinion of my dad: my mum has always said she would be happy to watch me open a tin of beans, but my dad is very honest and critical, and that is why I feel so grounded.

***

My mum thought it would be a good idea to put me into a competition called 'Search for a Star' at the Willows in Salford, and I passed all the heats and ended up in the final. It was very much like an old school cabaret club where you could have dinner and be entertained - they were really, really nice people. My mum went every week with our Sue to check my progress in the competition and I came first, winning £5K. I had just passed my test , (though I didn't pass first time, it took me two attempts, first fail was for positioning…!) and I went straight out and bought my first car, a blue Fiesta 1.3 Encore - I bought it from a Policeman. If you can't trust a policeman who can you trust! I was over the moon! I used to take it to nice places and take photos of it I was so proud. I eventually sold it to my dad's mate's daughter, who then bought another Fiesta off me after about four years.

Later on in my life I would end up with two cars, one in London and one in Liverpool. My second Fiesta was silver and the ST Model; all I needed was a Burberry cap and I was well blending in. I also had a brand new motorbike, a very cool Triumph Street Triple R. I remember being so proud of this bike that one day I came out of a London theatre to show it off to my mate - and it was gone! I looked down and there was my little disc-lock and chain lying there on the ground all by itself, where the bike was supposed to be: it was a very sad day.

Chapter 4

X Factor Auditions

I remember me and my mum one evening sitting and watching the X Factor over a Chinese; it was series two, the year that Shayne Ward won. From then on we watched the whole series right through from the auditions to the end, and we were glued to the final like millions of others around the country. Even though I had done so many competitions in my life, nothing compared to what looked so intense on the TV. When the winner was announced as Shayne Ward the volume on our set was almost up to max and Shayne's name echoed around our living room with the screams and cheers of the audience. I have to admit - I don't know if I was jealous or what! - but there was a little part of me that wanted to be in that position, and to be able to launch my career off that platform, but I never dreamed that twelve months later it would be me doing just that.

My mum turned to me and said, "You could smash that!"

"Yeah Mum, I know! I could do that definitely!" I said. Unbeknown to me, when applications were advertised my mum sent off for one and it landed on the doormat a couple of days later. "Aren't you going to fill it in then?" she asked.

"Oh my God, Mum what you doing? I was only havin' a laugh!"

She turned back to me and said, "I thought you were going to smash it?"

I just looked at her and smiled. To tell you the truth at the time I didn't think much else of it. I have always been that person not to over-think anything. The bizarre thing is that I didn't fill in the application, but a week or so later another application landed on the doormat with my mum saying, "What's this? Did you change your mind? We've got a second one now!"

"What! No!" I said. It was the day I returned with my dad from the second Dirty Dancing audition in my Ford Fiesta 1.3 Encore in blue (I loved that car) then a week or so later a third application form came in the post!

"Well, I'm making you fill this one out now, Son!" said my dad.

My nan, (God bless her soul) would always say, 'Things happen for a reason. Whatever is meant for you will not pass you by.' After my mum reminding me of this, and after I had asked my dad what he wanted for his Father's Day present, to which he replied, "If you really want to make me happy, Son, fill in that form for me and ya mum," I filled it out.

Some of the questions on the form I remember were like: What is your favourite animal? What's unique about you? Explain yourself in three words; do you play an instrument? What accent do you have? Do you have a stage name? Have you experience in TV, Theatre? Do you write music? Some of my answers were like, obviously, 'dog'. To explain myself in three words was the hard one - 'Confident, driven, ambitious.' I sent it off anyway, and on the same day I got my third recall for Dirty Dancing in London I got an invitation from X Factor to attend auditions at the Manchester United Football Stadium on 19th June 2006 at 08:00am.

That night X Factor was on the 10 o'clock News and the news caster was reading the story in an excited fashion. 'Thousands of people had already descended on the stadium and people were camping outside.' The TV showed images of loads of people already queuing in the stadium car park. My mum came into my bedroom all excited and woke me up. "Come on Ray, we need to get down to the stadium! People are already queuing for the auditions - there are thousands of them! If we don't get down there we won't get a place."

I was knackered at the time and just looked at my mother from my bed. "I can't be arsed going down there, Mum, and there is no way I am staying there all night. I don't think it's worth it," I moaned.

"Well, you stay in bed and me and our Sue will go down there and see what's happening." Mum seemed all excited, like it was a bit of an event, and with that they left the house. Twenty minutes later they called to say that there were thousands of people already at the stadium and some were camping out. Sod that! I thought. "Mum, don't be so ridiculous!" All the same my mum and our Sue said they would stay and save me a place in the queue and they would see me in the morning. I fell back to sleep and when I woke up I realised my mum and our Sue had indeed kipped out all night in the cold to keep me a place in the queue.

At about eight o'clock my dad gave me a lift down to the stadium. I remember it being bright and sunny, but it was still cold at that time of day, and I was still tired - I've never been one for getting up in the mornings. There were so many people it was unbelievable: I had never seen so many people in one place before, so how on earth was I going to be noticed amongst this lot! I had no style and was only wearing jeans and a Primark T shirt... I didn't know what I was going to do, but I did know what I was going to sing!

We called our Sue and she said she was in her pink coat by the burger van. It wasn't difficult to find her - her big pink duffle coat stood out like a beacon. My mother had to leave to go to work but my aunty was full of beans. They had stayed all night with a small tent they had packed in the back of the car, but they hadn't slept as it had been like a massive party, everyone all excited singing and dancing and generally having great fun. They had been talking to everyone around them and in particular a Welsh guy called Paul: apparently he was really nice. Bless him! I bet his ear was chewed off.

There were thousands of people in the area around the stadium. Some were enjoying the carnival atmosphere, singing and dancing and trying to draw attention to themselves as there were camera crews roaming around filming the crowd. My dad and I were in the queue a couple of hours before we got to the registration desk. When I gave them my details I was given a number - 30010 - which will stay with me for the rest of my life; mum has the very sticker framed and in her house.

Next we were ushered along and into the stadium seats overlooking the pitch. The stadium must have been three quarters full and the carnival atmosphere was still in evidence, with people dancing and singing. I sat with my dad wondering how they were going to audition all these people. There was another camera crew there, and someone with them asked everyone to cross their arms and shout out 'X Factor' as loud as they could. After they'd asked us to do this a number of times there were some moans from the crowd of 'Not Again!' and 'Why do we have to keep doing this!' I was used to repeating things a thousand times so I was quite happy doing it, but I turned to my dad and said, "How am I going to get noticed in this crowd, Dad? I don't think it's worth it. Shall we go home now, I'm starving!"

My dad turned and looked down at me, disgusted. "Listen ya little shit, your poor mother and our Sue have stayed out all night in the freezing cold car park to save you a place just so you could be here. If you want to go home Son, we can go, but you'll be disappointing me and letting your mother down. Just remember what your mum has done for you."

I quietly surrendered and with this we stayed. My dad is like my best friend and is a really good father to me: this is just how he speaks to me, or as he puts it 'speaks Scouse'

I saw the first of the auditions starting to take place in the distance. If you've ever been, you'll know the stands in the football ground are enormous and the pitch looked tiny from where my dad and I were sitting. I could see rows of people going along like a bus queue, standing in front of a man and then doing their bit of singing, some of them dancing along with it. Then the man would point up or down. It took an age to get to our row. I noticed one particular older guy a few rows in front of us; I don't know if he was there for the fun of it or just the experience. I watched as he got to the end of his row and was asked his name, which was Lionel Hutt. He sang a bit nervously, fluffed a line and then got a 'no' from guy in the production team. That was it for this guy Lionel: his X-Factor was over, along with thousands and thousands of others.

As the production team worked their way up the stadium towards where we were sitting a few rows back the man was saying "no," "no," "no," and there were people crying in every aisle. Some of them had come dressed up in bikinis or smart suits and it was freezing. My dad offered one girl his coat; she had hardly any clothes on and she was shivering. Much to his dismay she went off with it and we didn't see her for the rest of the day, so my dad sat there freezing instead. Then hours later she came running up from nowhere up and said thanks for the coat. She looked well happy, and so did my dad...he thought he had lost a coat!

There was no food allowed where were we sitting and we were starving. My dad was watching everyone's every move but I was quite oblivious. Then he said, "That bloke keeps looking at you Raymond - the same bloke that was saying 'no, no' to everyone. I looked down and my dad was right: this guy kept looking at me while he was auditioning the people in the rows below. After a while someone from the production team appeared at the end of our row and told all of us what was about to happen next. Each row of seats would line up and do an audition for the member of the X Factor production team; at this point you were either given a 'yes' or a 'no'. 'Yes' you went downstairs, if you got a 'no' you went up the stairs – a 'no' meaning that was your X Factor journey over and done with.

I felt my nerves begin to build and after the bollocking my dad had given me about what my mum and our Sue had done to get me there my legs felt weak, and I could feel the sweat starting to drip from my arm pits and down my sides. The man at the end of the row was in his early thirties and I now know him as Dan, who used to work for Sony and now manages Brian McFadden. By the time I finally got to the end I felt so scared I didn't know what to do. It was my dad that gave me a nudge with his knee and I stood there in front of this man ready.

"Hi! What's your name?" he asked.

"Hrrrr….me name's Ray."

"So what are you going to sing then, Ray?"

"'Ain't That a Kick in the Head' by Bobby Darren."

I sang and did a little dance. By 'dance' I mean I clicked my fingers a bit to keep in time with the song, (a technique I still haven't cracked!) The guy looked at me, paused for the longest breath known to man and said nothing, just pointed down. "Yes-ss! Come on, Son - you've done it!" Dad gave me a slap on my backside and off we went running down the 'Yes' tunnel, but then forgot to turn left as instructed, pushed through the double doors waving our arms in the air and found ourselves in the car park with all these cars and vans. "Quick, Ray! Grab the door! Shit....!" We were only lucky the emergency exit door was a slow closer, otherwise we could have been shut out. That would have been *so* embarrassing and God knows how we'd have got back into to the building. Nobody saw us, thank God, only all the technicians on the outside - probably thinking we were a couple of nutters.

When we finally found our way back inside we were so excited we were like a couple of headless chickens. We were given an orange strap and I was told to go down the stairs and find the Orange Area. At that very second Orange became my favourite colour. My dad and I headed down the stairs to an area in the stadium that was packed with people but now separated into coloured zones. We found the Orange Area and again waited. The wait was for another hour or so. We were both starving still, but there was no food or drink and this was incredibly draining on the both of us. Then I heard my name being called. I went up to the production assistant and asked if this was it, was I going to see Simon Cowell and the judges? She smiled at me and said that wouldn't be until a few days' time, and only if I got through the next audition. I asked my dad if he was coming with me and he looked at me and said 'No', and smiled and told me I would be ok on my own. The girl that took me through was really nice though, and made me feel confident. "They're really loving you," she told me. "They love that swing thing. Don't be scared! It's only the producers in there."

I was ushered into a room where a guy with ginger hair and a hard face who looked to be in his late twenties sat behind a desk. He was one of the producers of the show and asked me why I wanted to do this, what I would bring to the show. I had been scared of meeting the mighty Simon Cowell, but this guy was just as scary. I realised he was important, so I stood there and really sold myself with the pitch of a salesman: I was the product and I knew they wanted a product, so I sold myself as best I could. It was like a job interview for a high-powered job and this was my one chance to impress. He wrote down a load of notes and asked me to sing, so I sang 'Blue Suede Shoes'. He told me it was too upbeat and asked me to sing a ballad instead, so I sang 'Heartbreak Hotel'. I had all these off pat because of singing in the pubs. He then asked me to sing something else and in the end I think I sang five songs. Once I finished the last one he looked up at me with the faint hint of a smile appearing on his face and told me he was putting me forward to the next round. "I'm sure we'll see you again," he said. I never ever met this guy again.

I was given a pink slip and told to go downstairs to a registration desk where I would be given details for the next audition. They really check you out at this next interview; they asked me everything – whether I had a criminal record, about my health, my behaviour, if I was a good lad etc. and I had to fill out a load of forms. It was nine that night before we walked out to the car, and we didn't get home until gone midnight. That was one hell of a long day! Me and my dad stopped off for a bucket of KFC; we hadn't eaten since breakfast, and we were starving. There had been vending machines in the stadium but they had run out hours and hours before we even got to the inside. We got a big Family Bucket between the two of us and ate the lot – it was heaven, and I think to this day it was the best KFC I have ever eaten.

That night I soon as I got home I crashed into bed. I was done in.

Chapter 5

Lowry Hotel Auditions

The next audition was at the Lowry Hotel in Manchester. I asked my dad to go with me again, as my mum would just make me nervous; Kirsty, my girlfriend at the time and dance partner, came along too, to give me support. I had to turn up at ten am and then I had to register and go upstairs to a room with hundreds of people in it. I didn't know anyone until I spotted David Heath and the lads from Eaton Road. I walked over to him and asked him what he was doing there. "Same as you," he responded coldly. The other lads from Eaton Road were giving me daggers.

"Are you here as Eaton Road then?"

"Yes, we are. We've changed it to 'Eton' now, though, with no 'a'."

"Ahh… ok!" I had no other answer.

Then James Edwards added, "You were supposed to be here weren't ya……" and left it at that with a shrug of his shoulders.

What I found out later was that the lads felt I had let them down by not carrying on with the boy band thing. I didn't feel bad about it, though; I would never have been comfortable in a band, so with that I wished them luck and went and joined my dad and Kirsty, who were sitting at a table across the room. After a while some producers came out and mingled in the room and then came the camera crew. I was interviewed and had to explain why I was there, and what I wanted out of the X Factor. I told them I wanted to use this opportunity to show my talent, adding that once I was out there there'd be no stopping me. Again I was selling myself like a product. The camera crew moved away but kept homing in on me and I could see them filming me from the edges of the room. This interview was then used on the programme on the VT prior to my appearance on the TV show. After an hour or so waiting my name was called: Ray Quinn! I went up to the girl and asked if this was it. "Am I going to see Simon Cowell?" She told me no, that would be later; this was just some of the producers.

I walked in on my own, (my dad and Kirsty weren't allowed to come in with me) and there was a table with three people behind it – a brown-haired man in his late twenties and two ladies in their thirties, all casually but smartly dressed, and professional-looking. They told me they knew about my Brookside appearances and that I was not to mention it. If it was to come up later in the programme then they would deal with it. I was then asked why I wanted to be on the show, what I wanted to go on to be and what I could bring to the table. I was starting to get fed up with being asked the same questions, and because of it I didn't think I was giving as good a sales pitch as I had the last time. It was very frustrating. It felt like these people didn't talk to each other in between the auditions, as every time

I went into a room it was like I was being asked everything from the start again – how much did I want this? Did I want to win? How *much* did I want to win?' The usual questions were fired at me by all three on the panel. They took notes and conferred, and then after what felt like a lifetime they told me I was through to the next audition and I was to go back to the room and wait for my name to be called. As the day progressed the number of people in the room decreased. I was getting bored and tired sitting there - there are only so many glasses of water you can drink! Finally my name was called again and I went up to this lady and asked, "Am I going to see Simon Cowell now?" She smiled and nodded. So this was it! My stomach filled with butterflies: this was it, this was my chance!

When I walked into the room I could not believe what confronted me. What you don't see on the TV is all the cables and all the equipment, and there were so many people in there too. You don't end up auditioning in front of just three judges like you see on the programme; you audition in front of what must be a hundred others as well - sound men, lighting people, technicians, and directors - all sorts. I was asked to walk to an X on the floor, and as I walked in Sharon Osbourne said, "Hi, How are you Raymond?"

"Alright. How are you?" I answered, my stomach in my throat.

"Alright! So why are you here?"

"Well, I'm here to, er, do me best. Em, give 110%. Em, show you what I got, and...Em, hopefully get to where I wanna be."

"And where is where you wanna be?" Sharon asked,

leaning forward on the podium that the three judges were sitting on.

"Well, er, I er, I want….." I stumbled.

"Come on! You know!" Sharon encouraged me.

"I want everything, I want to be big. Once I get that break there'll be no stopping me."

"And who do you want to be like, Raymond?" Louis Walsh then asked.

"Er, I love Elvis. I love, er, Dean Martin, and I love Frank Sinatra, Bobbi Darren…"

"Good, good!" the judges were all saying and nodding in agreement. I could hear Sharon saying "Good boy." This was starting to feel great.

"I like all the big boys. Like, I want to be up there with everyone."

"Alright! So what are you going to sing?" Sharon asked with a smile.

I could feel my confidence building and at this point I think I might have been getting a bit cocky. I looked at the judging panel and smiled. "Well, something by someone I just mentioned actually. I'm going to sing 'Ain't that a kick in the Head' by Dean Martin'"

"Oi!" said Sharon, and "Good!" said Simon Cowell. This could not have been going any better and by now I was buzzing. I started busting out the tune along with some dodgy dance moves. I was loving it! At the end of the song Sharon gave me a little clap. I love Sharon - she is such a lovely lady, and I've met her again a few times since the X Factor. "I love you Raymond" she said, then smiled and turned to the other judges.

At this point Simon stepped in. "You know I always think that boys your age doing this whole swing thing

My first Competition! – Best in Show! At Pontins

*My First Birthday – with my brothers Robin (left)
and Darren (right)*

can be a bit precocious, but actually it wasn't bad at all." My reaction to that was not what you might expect it to be, as at the time I did not know what precocious meant!

Louis joined in now with, "I think you're really good, Raymond. You have great potential and a great smile, and people are going to love you."

"But," put in Simon, "if you're going to sing those songs, you have to be really, really good and at the moment you are 'good'."

"I think you're a natural," said Sharon. "There are some people that have that gift for entertaining, and I think you are *absolutely* gifted. Very, very natural! Great face! Love you, absolutely love you!"

"Yes, or no?" Simon interjected.

"One hundred percent yes," stated Louis.

"And it's a yes from me," said Simon.

"Oh God, I hope you are in my category!" added Sharon, and I had to laugh out loud. "Please! Love you. Yes!"

"Thank you very much! Thank you." I said and then bounced out of the room, not realising at the time that Simon was giving me a round of applause. As I left I heard Simon call after me, "Well done!" and I called back, "Thank you, bye then!" over my shoulder.

When I got outside the room I was buzzing. I was met by the film crew to ask how it went and I told them, "Sound! I'm on top of the world!" Then I pulled up the number on my T-Shirt and said, "Thirty Thousand and Ten! Don't forget that number - I am Ray Quinn!" I couldn't have felt any better.

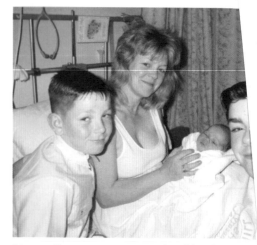

My very first appearance – one day old with my brot

This is me at ten weeks old in hospital with meningitis

My second cousin Stephanie was my very first dance partner, I am 3 years old here

Party time – age 5

*On my holidays with my mum
and dad*

*First public appearance – not
my best look!*

*Dance practice – I was
quite camp as a child!*

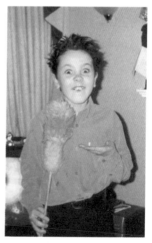

*My excellent impression of
our old neighbour Ken Dodd*

can be a bit precocious, but actually it wasn't bad at all." My reaction to that was not what you might expect it to be, as at the time I did not know what precocious meant!

Louis joined in now with, "I think you're really good, Raymond. You have great potential and a great smile, and people are going to love you."

"But," put in Simon, "if you're going to sing those songs, you have to be really, really good and at the moment you are 'good'."

"I think you're a natural," said Sharon. "There are some people that have that gift for entertaining, and I think you are *absolutely* gifted. Very, very natural! Great face! Love you, absolutely love you!"

"Yes, or no?" Simon interjected.

"One hundred percent yes," stated Louis.

"And it's a yes from me," said Simon.

"Oh God, I hope you are in my category!" added Sharon, and I had to laugh out loud. "Please! Love you. Yes!"

"Thank you very much! Thank you." I said and then bounced out of the room, not realising at the time that Simon was giving me a round of applause. As I left I heard Simon call after me, "Well done!" and I called back, "Thank you, bye then!" over my shoulder.

When I got outside the room I was buzzing. I was met by the film crew to ask how it went and I told them, "Sound! I'm on top of the world!" Then I pulled up the number on my T-Shirt and said, "Thirty Thousand and Ten! Don't forget that number - I am Ray Quinn!" I couldn't have felt any better.

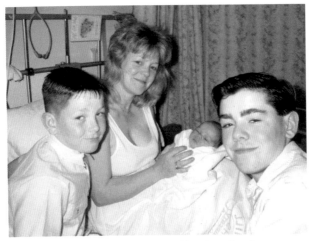

My very first appearance – one day old with my brothers

This is me at ten weeks old in hospital with meningitis

My first Competition! – Best in Show! At Pontins

*My First Birthday – with my brothers Robin (left)
and Darren (right)*

On my holidays with my mum and dad

First public appearance – not my best look!

Dance practice – I was quite camp as a child!

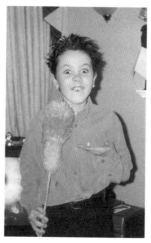

My excellent impression of our old neighbour Ken Dodd

My second cousin Stephanie was my very first dance partner, I am 3 years old here

Party time – age 5

Natalie and I in our first Disco dancing competition

Here we are again. Natalie and I, this time Ballroom

Julianne and I, this young lady went on to be a superstar in America

Winning trophies with my dance partner Bryony in the British Closed, Blackpool

Rocking the dance floor, Killing it I was!

Hanging out with the lovely girls – Natalie, Amanda and Julianne

Stacey and I posing for a picture before we hit the arcades!

The best dance partner that no one will ever beat – my nan

On the set of Brookside – the new family on the block

Brookside Life – love these people – Lindsey Muckle my mate sneaked in this shot she was not even part of Brookside (third from left)

Minty'- me on-screen Brookside dog. He was about 8 years old then. He was a really good dog and I swear he lived off Mars Bars!

This is part of the scene that led me to win my acting award

British Soap Awards 2002 - with me mum and Graham Norton. This is where I won 'Best Dramatic Performance'

At our house with me awards – 'Inside Soap Award' – 'Search for a Star award' and a couple of others!

Me on-screen parents who I will never forget - The wonderful Bernie Nolan who is no longer with us, I miss you dearly and of course the brilliant Neil Caple who gave me good advice that I still hold dear to this day

I met Louis Walsh at the Television Award Ceremony with me fat little face – little did I know we would meet again on the 'X Factor'

A big kiss for the most wonderful and kind woman, me beautiful nan. At a family party for our Robin's engagement

I was still dancing whilst in Brookside and this is me dance partner Kirsty, who later became me girlfriend – throwing some shapes on the dance floor – fake tan an' all!

Here I am 'Little Ray Quinn!' Callum on the left is still me best mate today and he is still taller and better looking – I hate going out with him!

Me and our Sue dancing around her place celebrating me award!

Me and me nan. I loved her very much, she was always the calm energy in the room unless she was having a heated discussion with me dad putting him and the world to rights! (God Bless her) x

Me and Kirsty. Me glamorous outfits that me poor mother put together – clever clogs she was!

Chapter 6

BOOT CAMP

Boot camp was a couple of weeks later and it was to take place over a few days at a large country house near Winchester on the 1st & 2nd of August, 2006. I had a letter instructing me to arrive the day before and saying that I was to get to Winchester station by five pm at the latest. At the end of the platform we would be met by Louise from the production team, who would be wearing an X Factor T-shirt. The letter explained there were two hotels and that the researchers would tell you which hotel you were in on arrival. I had to buy my own open return ticket and the letter told me it would be reimbursed.

My mum and dad dropped me off at Liverpool station and off I went. When I arrived I was met on the platform as the letter had stated. Luckily it was a nice day, as there were hundreds of us standing in a car park before being separated into two different groups, one for each hotel. Two coaches arrived, we were loaded on and off we went. The coach was the usual carnival, with people singing and everyone having a good time. I sat on my own and kept myself to myself. We were staying at a Travel Lodge, which seemed to be exclusively booked for the X Factor. I got my room and then had to go to a briefing.

At that briefing there were a number of people from the production team present. A guy named Ollie was in charge of telling us about the programme for the next few days. He informed us of some rules and regulations, what not to do, what not to say and what was going to happen; he also explained what would happen if we got through the auditions and what would happen if you did not. The room was full of excitement, with people clapping, and whooping and driving each other on. As infectious as it was, though, I didn't join in any of the whooping and hollering, just kept myself to myself for a bit. After the briefing was over we were allowed to choose some food from a table and told to chill out. We were told the times that each category would be collected the following morning. My category was scheduled for nine o'clock, which was early for me! Some of the contestants were in the bar that night but I went to my room and went to bed. As we were not allowed phones I couldn't call home or Kirsty. This was the first time I had been on my own with no contact to my friends or family, and it was exciting, but quite daunting. It was also going to be the first time I had to get myself up, and I like my sleep.

The following morning I was awoken by a bang on the door at the ungodly hour of eight o'clock, so I showered and made my way downstairs. There were a few people at breakfast that looked a bit the worse for wear. I remember thinking, 'Why would you tarnish an opportunity like this for a few beers!' and the talk that Neil Caple gave me came back to me. 'You have to stay professional at all times.' In my eyes, some of the contestants were not acting professional at this stage; I couldn't see these people going much further, as there were members of the production team watching us at all times, and some of them were at the breakfast watching everyone like hawks.

The mini bus arrived at nine. There must have been 24 people on my bus and we were taken to this big country house. It was very grand with a gatehouse and a long drive - it reminds me now of the house they use on Downton Abbey. When the bus pulled up at the front we were taken into the main reception area. There were hundreds of people all standing around; some were practising, most were just waiting for something to happen. Someone from the production crew told us to hold tight and wait for instructions, while around us the camera crews were still setting up. About an hour later some researchers came into the room and told us what was going to happen for the day, and then the camera crews started working around the room conducting interviews. It was a lot of hanging about, doing nothing.

I saw 'Eton Road' but didn't say anything to them and they did not talk to me. About an hour later I was interviewed by some researchers with a hand-held camera and microphone. They asked the usual questions. Did I have a game plan? How was I feeling? What was I going to do to impress the judges? I just regurgitated the answers I was now giving at every interview. I wanted to impress; I wanted to be given the opportunity to showcase my talents. We were given some sandwiches for lunch, and then in the early afternoon the under 25's were called to the lawn where we were to form as a group. One of the researchers told us that our mentor would arrive shortly and to hang tight. I knew Sharon Osbourne had a soft spot for me, so I was hoping it would be her. I didn't want Louis Walsh as my mentor: I thought if anyone was going to get me anywhere it would be Sharon or Simon; I don't have anything against Louis and what he does, but this was just the way I was thinking at the time.

We'd been stood outside for about twenty minutes before I heard the sound of a helicopter in the distance. Suddenly from behind the house appeared a blue helicopter which hovered above the group for a bit before landing in front of us, blowing dust and debris in everyone's face. The rotors started to slow, the door slid open and out stepped - Simon Cowell!

The group reacted in a mixed fashion. Some jumped with joy and others who'd been given a hard time by Simon through the auditions groaned, muttering things like, 'That's it for me! I'm going home,' already admitting defeat. I was quite happy it was him, so I was jumping up and down with everyone else in our group that was happy to see him. This was TV, so I played along.

Simon acknowledged the group, and then put his hand up to stop us from bouncing around and said, "I shall be watching you guys over the next couple of days. This is a massive opportunity for you, and I'm hoping to get the best out of you, so show me what you can do!"

With that he was escorted into the house.

***

Later on everyone was called into a room with Simon and Sinitta standing at one end with a big bald security guard. Simon made a little speech.

"All of you that have not auditioned yet, you have *got* to come in believing you can win! So far, most of you have come in as if you are half dead. The bad news is, because of that I am now doubling the number of people I'm going to send home. I was going to keep more but I have just changed my mind. I have seen just two people today with charisma – pathetic! So if you haven't got, it you might as well go home." 'Shit!' I thought. 'I need to smash this.'

After that, I remember standing in the room with five other contestants looking across to Simon Cowell and singing 'You're the Devil in Disguise' by Elvis. I was happy with my performance and from his reaction I think Simon was too. This was turning out a lot tougher than I thought it was going to be, though.

Now the auditions started in earnest. I was told to prepare an up-tempo song and a slow song and that I would be auditioned at 2:20pm. Just before I went in I met Kate Thornton for the first time. She seemed to be really nice and went out of her way to put me at ease. She asked me if I was nervous, and then said "Good Luck!" as I was ushered into a room where Simon Cowell and Sinitta were sitting behind a desk. They both said hello and then asked me what I was going to sing for them. My up-beat song was 'You're the Devil in Disguise' by Elvis. "That's no good. Give me something else," he told me.

This shattered my nerves and put me right off. 'Jail House Rock' was one of my bankers and he didn't like that either! I had to think fast and I went with 'Crazy Thing Called Love', which I managed to sing right through without him stopping me. After I'd finished - with no reaction from either of them – Simon asked me to sing my slow song. I sang 'Fly Me to the Moon', again to no reaction from Simon. He just said, "Thanks, Ray."

"Cheers!" I responded, and then left the room with no feedback from either Simon or Sinitta. I was met outside by a beaming Kate Thornton, who asked, "How did it go? How did it feel?"

"It went all right, yeah! I think I did ok - not much feedback, but I did ok," I answered, not really knowing what to think.

At the end of the first day they were going to tell us who was in the final 30. I remember the camera crew milling around the room filming people, and I was seen on the show stating I wanted to be in the final 30. We were called up to a room in groups. I think about 50 people were about to be sent home, and I was nervous but I believed I had done enough to get through. I remember going into the room with my heart in my stomach as Simon paused and then said, "You're through."

***

Next there was yet another round of interviews with the production team and I was asked how I thought my day went and what my plans were for tomorrow; we were then called together and put into groups of three. I was put with Stacey and Gathan and told that we would be expected to sing a song together.

After all that we were sent back to the hotel on the minibus. The cameras were still on us, and we had to learn these new songs they'd given to us, so I sat up late with the Gathan and Stacey. They were good singers and all for 'We have to do this! We have to be the best.' Which was good - they were driven like me! That night I went to bed late. Some of the other contestants were in the bar again, learning their songs with beer. It turned into a party for some and in the morning there was a bit of an altercation between a couple of the contestants as to who they'd slept with. Apparently the production team had to have words with some of them, but I was oblivious to any of this, just hearing it second hand on the bus on the way back to the house the following morning. Not that it concerned me anyway; I was just worrying about my performance and the day ahead.

I knew today was going to be hard, as I'd only ever sung songs that I knew. I'd never had to learn a song in a few hours and perform it, and this was really putting pressure on me. Gathan and Stacey were better than me at this stage; they had the song off pat but I was still struggling. We were going to sing Britney Spears' 'Baby, One More Time.'

Stacey stole the show and Simon saw this. When I look back now, I realise I just went with the flow and let myself be told what to do. I remember Simon laughing and saying in the audition, "You two were her backing vocals!"

I stood there like a lemon and said, "Oh, right!"

"That was what's known as a musical mugging," added Simon.

Sinitta laughed at this, on live TV too! "You two just got mugged big time!"

Stacey was a bit smug at this, and I did feel like I'd just been mugged off. I was not happy, and when we were interviewed by the production company afterwards I just didn't say anything. Stacey was on her high horse, and Gathan just sat there and let her speak. We were then told we were being whittled down to the final 14. I was first in with Stacy and Gathan and we were all put through. Again I felt confident for myself: I wasn't so sure about Gathan, but he made it.

After the group song they *then* told us we had to pick one of three songs from a list and be ready to perform it in an hour. I couldn't believe it! I didn't know any of the songs on the list, so I was back to square one of learning a new song and with less time to do it. By now my nerves were getting the better of me. I was in panic mode. I'd decided to sing 'Easy' but although I was familiar with the song, I didn't know the words, so I was walking endlessly around the garden trying to get them learnt. I had a piece of paper with the lyrics on it, and I was trying so hard to get the song in my head. At this stage of my career I had never had to learn a song in such a short time. Then I started to notice that people were being told to leave; the number of people in the house was getting smaller and before I knew it, it was my time to go in for the audition. I was not prepared, though; I was very scared - and scared of failure. I did not want to let myself down when I had got this far.

I remember walking into the room, standing on the spot and just starting to sing. I got as far as the first line of the song and then it went completely out of my head. I hummed along for a bit and then stopped singing: I had lost it completely. I stood there, looked at my feet and said, "Sorry, can I please use the words?"

Simon nodded and I pulled the piece of paper with the words on it out of my back pocket. "So sorry!" I said again, shaking my head as I unfolded the paper, and then just started singing again. I finished the line and tried to smile, tried to show I had confidence. I looked at Simon and he was sitting there with his hand to his face. He just looked at me and said, "Thanks." Sinitta had a big smile but Simon didn't look too happy.

I said thank you, and left the room feeling gutted. I was met outside by Kate and the production team. "I blew it!"

"No! Did ya?" said Kate.

"Totally - just blew it! I let myself down big time. I know I can do better." Kate patted me on the arm.

I left the camera crew and went and found a corner and just sat there in a ball. One of the researchers asked me if I was ok and if I wanted a glass of water, which I turned down. I just wanted to be alone. I felt like this was it. I had blown it, and how was I going to tell my mum! The others were sitting there too waiting for their interviews, but I just tried to keep myself to myself. When I was eventually called up to see Simon and Sinitta I climbed the stairs with dread. I was met by Kate, who wished me luck, and then I was ushered in. Simon and Sinitta sat behind the desk and Simon asked me, "How are you?"

"I feel like I've have just let myself down."

"What I love about you, you have great confidence, but…."

"But…." I said, guessing what he was about to say. My stomach just felt like it was a bag of butterflies.

"The singing, particularly today on the last song, has let you down. The decision is, you haven't made the final seven. I'm really sorry."

With those words I felt my world crash around me. I couldn't help it, but the tears flooded my eyes. "I said I wouldn't cry," I told no one in particular as the camera was focused on me. I left the room not wanting to speak to anyone. I didn't know what to do with myself: I had to go back home now and tell my mum I had failed. I was beside myself, the last thing I wanted was to be on camera with Kate interviewing me, and they led me down the stairs into the library to calm down, knowing no one was in there. Everyone else was gone by now and so I was on my own. Then Kate came into the room followed by a camera crew some time later. "Ray can you come with me?" she asked, grabbing my hand and leading me back upstairs. "Simon wants to see you."

Back in the audition room I asked Simon if he wanted me to stand on the stage again. "Look, I'm sorry Ray to be putting you through this, so I'll make it short and simple. I've changed my mind. You're through."

I couldn't believe it! A minute ago it was all over, and I was wondering how I was going to tell my mum - now this. "You're joking me? Sound!"

Simon and Sinitta laughed and I went over to Simon to give him a hug. "Ray, don't let me down."

"I won't."

"Alright, Kiddo!"

I left the room ecstatic. I had made the final eight.

Chapter 7

Judges' House

This was it! I was down to the final eight. I turned eighteen on 25th August 2006 and this was the date any contractual agreement with Mrs Byatt finished. The fact that I had signed with her until the age of eighteen had all been checked during the early rounds of X Factor and it was agreed that by the time the Judges' Houses started I would be out of contract. A letter had come through saying, 'Congratulations on getting this far, and Simon is looking forward to seeing you in Miami for the Final Audition Stage.' The letter told me I would be flying from Heathrow Airport, Terminal 3 on Wednesday 6th September, and I was to meet Lisa and Oli at 7:30am at the Virgin Air Desk in the Departure Hall. 'Please DON'T BE LATE,' it said. 'Please only buy one-way tickets as we will be arranging your travel home, and remember to bring receipts. Lisa and Oli will be ringing you beforehand for all your travel details.' We were to be spending three days in Miami and must take three changes of on-camera outfits.

My mum drove me down and we stayed near Heathrow the night before. These early mornings were killing!

As arranged, I was met at Heathrow by Oli and Lisa and the five other contestants, who were Leona Lewis, Shaun Rogerson, Stacey Barnes, Nakita Angus, Ashley McKenzie, Gemma Sampson and Carlo Muscutelli. I was all excited, but Mum told me she was going to miss me; she was quite worried having to leave me with Oli and Lisa! Anyway, I was left in the capable hands of the X Factor production team, and we checked in and went through to Departures to await our flight. We were all sitting about together, drinking coffee, tea and having breakfast. We weren't allowed our phones, as no one was allowed to know the results.

We all flew over Coach Class; it was a nine hour journey and I couldn't sleep, so I just watched the in-flight films. We went through Customs at the other end, and this was it - I was in Miami, on my own. This was so exciting for me. A coach arrived to take us to the hotel and when we got there we were briefed about what was going to happen. There was nothing scheduled until the next morning, so the rest of the day and the evening was ours. I was sharing a room with Shaun Rogerson. He was a quiet, nervous little guy but we got on well, and the hotel was great: at that time the best I'd ever stayed in. We put our bags in the room and then went to the swimming pool, where the rest of the contestants joined us, all wanting a tan. The heat was unbearable, and I wasn't used to it so I went for a walk with Shaun to explore. We went to Muscle Beach and then grabbed a proper American McDonalds. The waitress behind the counter asked me in a really strong American accent where I was from and what was my accent. I told her I was from Liverpool and she asked me if that was like the Beatles. I was made up! Shaun then went off and did his own thing and I kept myself to myself for the rest of the day. I went in search of some Heelys too. I was at that in-between age, a child in some ways and an adult in others. Anyway, I found some, bought them and then heeled my way all the way back to the hotel. I was buzzing! That night the production team took us out for a pizza in an Italian up the road from the hotel. I had my Heelys on and I was loving my life.

The following morning we were collected at nine and taken to Simon's house, which was on the coast line along a huge private road lined with palm trees and with security gates restricting access. The house was like something out of a film. We pulled up outside and no one on the bus could believe it! Oli turned round to us and explained, "This is very exclusive area for the rich and famous, all A-listers from film, sports and music. I know you have your cameras on you but if you see any, you are not allowed to ask them for an auto-graph or a picture. You are here for one reason only." Then he added. "Also do not take any pictures of the house – not the outside and definitely not anything in-side, Ray!" With that he smiled, we all agreed and then we were led in.

We were shown all round before the cameras were set up. The house was stunning, with huge, gorgeous gar-dens and a huge front door like a church door, and outside there was a gorgeous infinity pool overlooking Miami. This was where I wanted to be; this was the life style I wanted to aspire to. As I walked around I soon realised there were no pictures of Simon anywhere in the house. I asked Oli. "Is this even Simon Cowell's house?" Oli turned round to me and put his finger to his lips as if for me to be quiet. All the time I was there I kept asking him if it was Simon's house and on the last day before we left he said, "No. We think its Tom Cruise's, though."

After the guided tour we had to leave the house and wait outside, where we sat about drinking cans of coke. It was roasting, and all the girls were on the lawn trying to get a tan. There was a long time of doing nothing while the production team were busying themselves with the schedule. We just hung about waiting for something to happen. We had been given our song choices two weeks before going to Miami, and I had chosen a Robbie Williams track 'She's the One', and 'Smile'. We had a half-hour each with a session pianist, a really nice chap in his early thirties. He liked my version of 'She's the One', but said that 'Smile' was a bit drony as it was, and he wanted to try something else. He sprung on me this other version of 'Smile' that had a key change at the end and was up in tempo. I hadn't practiced it like that, or worked with this pianist before, so I had to learn the new version in half an hour to be ready for my audition. He told me I sounded great, so I asked him if he thought it was what they were after and he said that it probably was. This filled me with a lot of confidence. I was impressed with his playing too, he was a talented musician.

After this, I had to go and wait for my audition to sing my first song. Everyone was sitting in the lounge and we could see the camera being set up by the pool and Simon and Sinitta making their way down there. We were called out one by one, and then taken into a holding room, so we couldn't see the other contestants' performances. Then we were taken to various parts of the house to be recorded doing interviews, and once the interviews were over were sent back to the lounge. It seemed like an age before anything happened. We all just sat in this lounge chatting, and then being taken one by one to audition. Once called for the audition the contestant did not return. I was called fourth out of the six of us.

When my turn came I was told to wait at a spot just outside the pool area, then Kate Thornton appeared and I had to do an interview with her. She told me that they were going to film me and ask me how I was feeling and whether I felt confident. The audition followed straight after the interview, and I was called forward to appear in front of Simon and Sinitta. Simon asked me what I was going to sing. I found this strange, as I would have thought that he would have chosen my songs, or at least known what they were, but this was TV and I was used to it. I sang 'She's the One' and I didn't think it went very well; it certainly wasn't the best I could do. Simon just sat there and then said "Thank you" and that was it! I went back to Kate Thornton and she asked me, "How did it go? How do you feel? Do you think you've done enough to get through?"

Well, I felt a bit numb and that's what I told her. I didn't feel as if I'd done what he had wanted.

Outside the house I was joined by the other contestants once they had done their auditions. We all conferred and asked each other how it had gone for each of us. Everyone said they had done really well. I was the only one who didn't seem too pleased with my performance, and this made me re-think everything and perhaps over-think a little bit. I was sure I had blown my chances at the first hurdle, and knowing I would have to nail the next song, I could feel my nerves coming back. Soon we were ushered back into the house for Round Two, and this was for the version of 'Smile' that had been given to me no more than a few hours ago.

The second audition followed the same pattern as the first. We had to go off to meet new interviewers, and then were called one by one to be interviewed by Kate Thornton, who asked the same sort of questions. 'How did the last one go? What are your thoughts on this one?' All the while you are being filmed you are turning into a bag of nerves and beginning to lose confidence in yourself! I tried to keep myself positive, though, and not to start doubting my ability.

There I was, then, standing in front of Simon Cowell and Sinitta again and shaking with nerves. The pianist did his introduction to the song and this was it. This was my final chance to impress. I could hear my dad in my head. 'Smash it, Son, you can do this!' Then I heard my cue to start and I gave it my best – I *did* smash it! – and I was really proud of myself. I looked at Simon and he just said, "Thanks Ray" with no emotion, but I knew in myself that I had done my best and I had not let anyone down.

One of the runners then came and took us to an out-of-the-way part of the house and told us to sit tight. We waited again for what seemed like an age. At this stage we speculated that we might have the results today and

Oli had told us if that happened we would have a day off tomorrow. A couple of hours later it was getting dark outside when Oli arrived in the room and told us there was going to be no decision tonight as Simon wanted to sleep on it. We were to do another round of interviews and then it would be off back to the hotel. It was late by the time we got in and I went straight to my room. Shaun was already there and we had a chat about the day's events, I couldn't really sleep that night. The whole day was playing on my mind - the performances, the interviews, what the other contestants had said about their performances: it had all been very draining.

The next day we were picked up at the same time and then taken to the house. We were outside again sitting about not doing a lot and I wandered to the front gate. As I was looking out onto the deserted street this enormous man with two Alsatian dogs suddenly appeared. He was wearing white T-Shirt, bullet proof vest and blue combat trousers with loads of keys attached to the belt. I suddenly recognised him: it was Shaq O'Neal the famous basketball player. I was a big fan, so I said hello to him and he walked over. He asked me what I was doing there and when I told him he nodded and said, "Yeah, English TV, I know! They're renting the house off Tom." I asked him what *he* was doing and he told me he was a Deputy, paid to look after the neighbour. He showed me the badge on his bullet-proof jacket, which I thought was really cool. When he shook my hand, his hands were like shovels and dwarfed mine. I was made up to have met him, and it took my mind off what I was doing. When I re-joined the group and told them all excitedly that I had met Shaq O'Neal and had shaken his hand, they turned to me and said Shaq who?!

The camera crews were busy setting themselves up and we didn't see anything of Simon until we were being auditioned. I don't know what part of the house he and Sinitta were staying in, but we were kept well clear of it. We put in a room together and told that we would have to wait a little longer, as Simon had still not made a decision. Ashley piped up and asked, "How long do you think it'll be? How long until he *does* make a decision? How much longer will we have to wait?"

"I don't know," Ollie answered. "Could be half an hour, could be a couple of hours. Just sit tight! You'll soon find out."

So we sat around for a couple more hours with nothing to do, until finally one of the production crew came into the room and told us that Simon had made a decision and the result was final. We were told that we were going to be interviewed (again!) and would then be taken through to meet Simon to get the results. By this time it had all become overwhelming; we had just got so used to waiting around. All I had in my head was that I didn't want to be getting on that plane with a 'no' result.

I was called away to speak to Kate Thornton, who asked the *same* questions. "Results are in! Do you think you have done enough? Are you nervous? How would you feel if he said yes?"

As I looked at her I was thinking to myself, well what do you think? What would you be thinking? It's such an emotional strain to go through this kind of competition; everything is monitored and it gets to you in the end. There's no let up from the intensity.

There we were, sat in a room again with the contestants being called out one by one, and you couldn't hear anything that was going on outside. It was such a strange atmosphere and all of us in there were so young - most of us under the age of twenty. This was a monumental step: your future life hanging on the decision of one man. I was one of the last two left in the room, the other being Leona, and we discussed what was about to happen. I asked her if she was hopeful; she simply said "I have done what I could." When I got called out I turned to Leona and said, "Good luck! I hope you get through," and with that I left the room.

I was sent over to where I did the audition and had to stand in front of Simon Cowell. He looked at me for a moment and then said, "It's taken me a long time to arrive at this. You're the one that got me baffled because your first song wasn't great, and you have got me worried because I have taken a chance on you. I was back and forth and back and forth with a decision that I am now happy with. You brought yourself back with the second song, but still there was an element of doubt. But I *have* now definitely made up my mind. You are in my final four, Kid." With this he smiled.

"You're joking!"

"No, I'm not."

"Oh, my God!" I said, putting my hands up to my head. This is start of an amazing opportunity, I thought to myself. I was in tears. I'd done all the hard stuff – now it was up to the public to judge me.

He came over to hug me and slapped me on the back. Then he said, "Off you go, Son!"

One of the production team called me forward and I ran over to give them my initial reaction to the result on film. Kate Thornton was there too and I gave her a big hug. I kept saying, "I can't believe it! I can't believe it!"

Kate smiled. "Believe it, Ray – you're going through!"

I went outside, looking for everyone. They were all hanging about, and the atmosphere was really strange. We were all together and yet of course some had got through others hadn't. Some were really emotional and I remember Shaun saying in his strong Yorkshire accent, "Tell you the truth, I'm glad I didn't get through, I don't think I could cope much more with the emotion of it all. I'm glad it's over - I get so bloody nervous!"

After we got back to the hotel by mini bus I spent the night talking with Shaun, who was telling me what he was going to do next and how he was going to do things differently.

The flight back was another early flight. The camera crew were on the plane and even though we were in Economy Class, we were interviewed in First Class with a glass of champagne, talking about how we were feeling. Once the interview was over we were sent back to Economy! The four of us that had been put through were all hyper on the flight; the four that hadn't were just sitting in their seats with the headphones on. When I arrived back at the airport in London I was driven up to Liverpool so that no press could get close to me. The X Factor is a big show in the UK and the press want to get any story they can about it, so they were all keeping a close eye on the contestants, looking for any gossip or exclusives.

I was driven up to Liverpool in a car with one of the contestants that didn't make it through from Woolton, which was only around the corner from where I lived. We spoke briefly in the car, but I was not really paying attention as I was so excited to tell my family I was through.

My mum had already been contacted by the production team and told she was allowed a maximum of six people in the house. A camera crew turned up and was waiting for me when I arrived, and my mum, our Sue, my dad, uncle Steve and Kirsty were all there to greet me. When I walked into the house I had to wait on the stairs for about fifteen minutes while the production team made sure everyone was in the right position in the Garden. While I was sitting on the stairs I was thinking, how shall I play this? Shall I act all sad as if I didn't get it, or should I just come out with it with a big cheesy grin? Then I was asked if I was ready, and with that I had to go into the garden.

I went in with my head down, but I was so excited that within a millisecond I told them. "Yeah, Baby!" and threw my hands up in the air. My dad ran over and dived on me with his legs wrapped around me. He turned to the camera with a big grin on his face, hands in fists. Then my nan comes over to me and I give her a big hug. I am glad that scene is on the VT as my nan was with me through all my early career.

Chapter 8

X Factor Finals

Now I was in the live finals I had to go down to the Fountain Studios in London with everyone else who had been put through. We were all sitting on stands scattered around the walls when someone from the TV studio came in to explain what was to be done next. After giving a speech about it being good to have us there, and saying well done for getting this far they explained there were a number of legal documents and some other paperwork needing to be signed to ensure our welfare on the show.

"We have a legal team here that can help you with the documents. Have a read through first, and if you have any questions or queries that is what they are here for. Again, congratulations for getting this far and good luck for the rest of the show."

After that we were snowballed with paperwork, and there were a lot of questions being asked. I had never had a contract put in front of me like this before and I didn't know where to start. I asked a few of the other contestants what they thought of it, and someone explained that I was going to be appointed a manager, a tour manager, and I was not allowed to have any other management. There was also a binding clause that said I was not allowed to do anything for three months after I finished the X Factor.

It was explained that before anyone went any further all the documentation needed to be signed. It was to protect them and us if anything should arise during our time in the show. After a while I thought, well, I must be in safe hands, so I'll sign. We all took our documents into another room to be witnessed and signed, and once this was done, spirits picked up again and everyone started to practice in small groups.

Before I knew it I was moving into the X Factor House.

***

The house was in Wembley in London. It was huge, with a massive living room, kitchen, gym, garden and six bedrooms. We all arrived together on a bus and were told to have our hoods up so we wouldn't get papped. When we got inside a member of the production team told us which rooms we were in. We didn't have a choice of who we shared with, but I was with Ashley McKenzie and Robert Allen, and we all got on. Eton Road were in the house with me too, as they had reached the Finals by default; they hadn't made it through the original Judge's House but got into the Live Finals because the original band 'Avenue' that *had* got through had been kicked out due to contractual issues. It was reported in the press that the band had been put together by an ex-producer from the X Factor who had no association with the show any more, and they had a contract. (I don't know the full story; as far as I was concerned it was all hear-say.) So - Eton Road was 'in the House'! I had known these lads for years, but they still had a grudge against me for pulling out of the band, and we didn't gel as if we were the best mates we used to be. I'd known David for years when I was younger, and James was dating Natalie, my old dance partner, before splitting with her and forming a relationship with David a while later. I don't know when this relationship started but looking back on it now, the signs were all there.

The house was full of artists, all vying for attention. To start with there was a lot of friction that would boil up and then cool down. On some days you could cut the tension with a knife. Some were better at handling it than others, I just kept myself to myself and kept my head down. The tension in the house seemed to get less as the competition went on and contestants were removed from the house. There was more space and you could keep yourself to yourself.

I remember Ben Mills' cowboy boots, though - everyone complained about the smell of these. They would stink the whole place out - they were horrible! We all had to muck in to clean the house, and there were certain rules, such as 'If you get it, put it away; if you use it, clean it.'

I remember one time at dinner and Anthony Harris from 'Eton Road' wolfed down a massive warm chicken Caesar salad. I turned to him and said, "Mate, you did well there. I couldn't have finished that myself. It was massive. I tell you what," I said cheekily, "that's the most I've ever seen you eat!"

At that he stood up without hesitation and said, "I did enjoy it, yeah, you patronising cunt!" and then stormed out. The rest of 'Eton Road' were looking at me disgusted, as if I shouldn't have said that. What I didn't realise at the time was that Anthony had an eating disorder. The guy was really skinny and this was honestly the most I had seen him eat. I had known these guys for years, but they still held a grudge against me for not joining the band. I couldn't see what they were so pissed off about, they were in the same stage of the competition as I was, though they had just scraped in. But saying that, so had I. So we were in the exact same boat.

On the day after moving into the house we were given our first song, lyrics and a cd. We were never given a choice of what song we would sing and I wasn't happy about my first week's number - 'Ben' by Michael Jackson, which presented me in a light I didn't want to be seen in. I would never have challenged the choice of song, but it took some convincing. As the weeks rolled on we used joke about the songs we were given. Sometimes we were happy, other times we just thought, 'are you messin'!'

We went to rehearse in a recording studio near Chelsea. This was where I first met Yvie Burnett, who was to be my voice coach with Mark Hudson; they were both eccentric characters and Mark had a multi-coloured goatee. I got on really well with both of them. The rehearsal was being filmed, and Yvie and Mark asked me if I had heard the song before and if I was happy with the song choice. I said yes, but then when I'd sung it for the first time I told them, "I'm not so sure about this song. I really don't know if it's the one for me."

They just said, "Well, it's a cute song. It'll do you good for Week One."

I hate the word 'cute' - never liked it! The only thing cute in my world is my little boy 'Harry', and he wasn't about in those days.

During the week I had to go to Wardrobe to discuss my 'look', and when they asked me what I normally wore I answered, 'Clothes'.

The wardrobe lady laughed and said, "No, Silly! What *sort* of clothes do you wear?"

From this moment on I was known to her as Cheeky Little Quinny. She was a lovely friendly lady and we would always have a bit of a laugh together. Anyway, I told her I normally wore suits to my gigs, so from then on they put me in suits.

On other days I had to do PR and speak to the press and big the show up. We had a day dedicated to all of us when we went into a room at ITV and met the press. They would be there with their microphones and recording devices, cameras flashing and asking questions. It was fun though, and another thing to get used to. One day I did enjoy was when they took me to a posh hair salon in London where I was re-styled. It would have easily cost more than £200 if I had gone into there as a normal punter. The one thing that I was not expecting was my eyebrows to be plucked and since then I have to do it regularly as they grow back like bushes now. My scalp was massaged with menthol conditioner; I had my hair dyed and my hands manicured. It was like something off the TV, but then again I realised I *was*!

The first live show was on the Saturday at the Fountain studios in Wembley, North West London, and I had been rehearsing all week. We were due there at around eight am, as we all had a slot to do sound checks. On week one there was a lot of us, so sound checking took quite a while. This was the first time we had seen the studios and it all seemed so small to what you saw on the TV. Like with a lot of things in life, the reality didn't live up to expectations.

I remember being asked what I wanted to be known as. Was it Ray or Raymond, as this was what would be going on the big screen. I had to phone my mum and ask her what I should be called. She just said, "Whatever you think is best."

"Mum, I'm asking you!"

"Well, Raymond then."

So I told the visual engineer guys, call me 'Raymond.' We were there all day and had our lunch in this really nice canteen. I do enjoy my food and having a good canteen was a bonus. The day was spent rehearsing with the voice coaches, wardrobe, doing interviews for the VT for the programme and hanging around the Green Room. Once again I didn't feel confident with the song choice, but everything else felt right and I told myself I just needed to go out and smash this. You could sense the different vibes from different people: Ashley was over confident and full on, whereas the McDonald brothers were worried and not confident at all. They told me they were not used to big spectacle stages like this, with all the lights and razzmatazz; Craig was always full of nerves before their appearance, and he would always disappear for twenty five minutes before he went on stage, I remember being with his brother Brian one night on the show and asking him where Craig goes. He looked at me and smiled. "Taking a crap, Mate!" in a strong Glaswegian accent.

That night all of us were in the Green Room watching the show live on the TV. The first act was the 'Unconventionals'. I was one of the last acts on that first night and was called out of the Green room about ten minutes before I had to appear on stage. After they'd done the final checks on my microphone I was told to stand behind the right-hand doors. I remember Simon saying, "Please welcome my next act – from Liverpool, the fantastic Raymond." The doors opened and I felt full of confidence. This was where I wanted to be, this was where I saw myself, and it felt natural for me to be here. When the music started I couldn't help thinking, 'Not this song!' but then I just did it to the best of my ability. The atmosphere in the room was electric.

The worst part of the night was standing on stage waiting to hear whether you had got through to the next round, and the worst thing that could have happened was to be out on the first week. It was the 'Unconventionals' that were out though, after doing a sing off with Deon Mitchel. I remember my name was called early as being safe, so I joined Simon Cowell on stage and he gave me a hug and a slap on the back. I was surprised that we hadn't had much contact with Simon so far; I'd only seen him once the first week – just briefly on the Friday, when he asked me, "How are you Ray, and how are you feeling?" I told him I was fine and excited, and that although I hadn't been sure about the song at first, I was happy with it now.

He answered, "You'll be fine Ray! It's a good song, and it's Week One." And with that he left.

On the show he was called our mentor, like the other judges for the other contestants, but we saw little of them, and there was no mentoring going on. I had my coaches but no word of a pep talk from Simon. I realise though, that he must be a very busy man.

After the show all the families were in the Green waiting for all us contestants to go down. We got our first drink free. I remember my dad telling me, "You were fantastic, Son, absolutely fantastic, and you looked boss in your suit. But one thing, Son - change the name!"

"Why's that, Dad?" I asked.

"Ray Quinn sounds better than 'Raymond'. You need your second name in there, Son."

With that I changed it from the second week on.

The highs of the next few weeks for me were in my confidence building. It was fun to be in the media limelight, and go to red carpet events and be like a star. By Week Three I was well into my comfort zone, as it was Big Band Week and I got to meet Tony Bennett. I was buzzing! I got on really well with Tony Bennett and he invited me to his gig in the Royal Albert Hall later that year. Things could not have been better for me.

Week Five brought my confidence crashing down around me though, as I was in the bottom two with Nikitta. The theme of the week was love songs, and in my view I gave one of my best vocal appearances on the show with 'Crazy Little Thing Called Love'. It really shocked me that I was in the bottom two. I had to sing the same song again and I didn't feel confident, but I had no choice but to go for it. I remember Sharon voting for me, Louis voted for Nikitta and

Simon dragged it out a bit, telling the audience he had changed his mind, at which they all gasped. I thought he was about to put Nikitta through, but then to my relief he gave me yet another chance, and that was the last time I was in the bottom two. I remember someone associated with Nikitta came up to me later and said "Well done Ray, you were both fantastic tonight – but you do know really that Nikitta should have gone through!" This was my first taster of just how intense this competition was, especially as Nikitta was a real good friend at the time. I just shrugged the comment off and carried on.

The press attention on what Simon had said that night about changing his mind was colourful to say the least, and in those days there was no Facebook or Twitter. I think Simon's input helped me in the competition, as I had a lot of additional media attention that week. Top Man, Simon!

As the weeks went on the house got emptier and emptier, until by Week Six I had a room of my own, which was nice. In the final two weeks it was down to Leona, Ben and me, but by this stage Ben had upset a number of producers about song choices and artistic differences and had been very vocal on the Winner's Single, stating that it was more geared towards Leona. The Powers that Be had to visit the house one evening and they took him into the kitchen and shut the door. I wasn't aware of what was said but no one came to chat to me. That week was the last week for Ben: he was voted off the show and it was Leona and myself in the final.

Those last few days were crazy. I had four songs to

learn and one of them, a ballad, was brand new. I had to go to Liverpool that week, to visit the Met Quarter Shopping Centre, which was amazing. The support was incredible – there were thousands of people there. I had to do loads of radio interviews, and I had to visit my old school Rudson, where all the kids went mental. I noticed the flyers that were stuck up all over Liverpool too, this mainly down to my mum and our Sue! I then had to record the single, which I did at a separate time to Leona, and it was awful. The song was a ballad and I had been singing swing the whole time. Leona had been singing the ballads. Once the single was recorded I was given a copy though, as was Leona. I remember one night I was listening to my track in my room thinking, 'I don't suit this song, I'm not a pop star. The song's good but it's not me.' Then I went next door to where Leona was listening to her single and listened at the door. I thought mine was sound, but hers was unbelievable! I knew then I wasn't going to win, but I was still more than happy to have got to where I had in the competition.

On the day of the Final I was doing my sound check and Louis Walsh was watching. When I'd finished and walked off stage I bumped into him and he told me, "You sounded fantastic – you've done a great job! Are you looking forward to getting out there?"

"I can't wait! I'm going to go out there and give it some welly, and I'm just feeling lucky that I've got to this stage. In my mind, no matter what the result is, I have already won."

To which he replied, "Ray, just go out there and have fun - and enjoy it, Ray, enjoy it!" And then he added,

"You know Simon is going to sign you anyway. So just enjoy it."

"Is he?" I asked. "He hasn't said anything to me yet!"

This gave me a bit of reassurance and comfort that the show was not about to end. There was a pot of gold at the end of the rainbow.

It was the night of the final and the media hype was massive, with an estimated 13 million people going to watch the show, and they had outside broadcasts for both Leona and me. There were a few hundred in the Apollo Theatre in Liverpool on a live feed. The presenter was Jeff Brazier, and Leona Lewis had Myleene Klass at the Hackney Empire. The media had been full of the X Factor all week; this was such a big show at the time. I had to sing a song with 'West Life,' who had a Swing /Big Band album out at the time of my X Factor, so it seemed natural for the producers to team me up with them on the night. I only met them on the day of the final and was only given one rehearsal with them. They were really nice lads and very professional, and I have a lot of respect for them. Leona sang with 'Take That,' minus Robbie Williams.

I was first to perform. I just went for it, and as Louis Walsh had advised, I enjoyed myself. The night was electric and the crowd was immense. It was just awesome. Shaun Rogerson made a special appearance on the night. I think it was the first time I have seen him sing a song all the way through. Nothing went wrong, and the swing performances went well. I was looking forward to singing the final single, but when I got out on stage and performed it, it just did not feel right. In my mind I knew I had lost the race. Leona followed my performance and she was just insane! After the show was done, we had to wait while Coronation Street was aired and the votes were counted. During the break Simon Cowell came up to the two of us and said, "You both did a fantastic job. Best final so far!"

Leona said. "Thank you" and walked off.

Simon turned to me. "I'm telling you now, Ray, this final could go either way."

It was reported in the press up north that the Telephone Exchange in Liverpool crashed on the night of the voting, due to being overwhelmed with calls. Whether this affected the result I will never know, but the support they gave me on the night is a credit to the people of Liverpool.

Coronation Street finally finished and the warm-up act came off stage. The judges were called on set and then Leona and I were called. "Please welcome to the stage the last two remaining acts in our Grand Final, the 16-24 Category!" The doors opened and the crowd went wild as we walked down to centre stage. We stood there and held hands. Kate Thornton then wished us both luck and announced that eight million people had voted. Then she said, "And the winner of X Factor 2006 is…." There was short pause. "Leona!" The crowd went mad, the auditorium erupted, and Kate added that Leona was the first woman to win the competition.

I lifted her off her feet and said, "I told you, didn't I!"

Leona was speechless, and there were tears in her eyes. Simon joined us on stage and I said to him, "I told her before!"

Simon spoke in my ear. "Ray, you couldn't have done

any more. I'm going to give you a career." Then he shook my hand.

I turned to Leona and said, "Can you believe it, Baby!" She was just squealing with excitement and all smiles. Kate Thornton asked the familiar question, "How are you feeling Ray?"

I answered, "Well… weird. I'm so happy for Leona, she's done amazing. And she's the first girl to win X Factor too - how about that?" I turned to Leona, "Well done, Baby!" and she gave me a hug. Kate asked Simon Cowell what he would like to say to Ray. "I got to hand it to this guy, he came in! He was the underdog for a while, and then came in as joint favourite, maybe slightly ahead. Couldn't have asked more of you, Ray! As I have said before, you have something special: it's called the likeability factor."

When I left the stage all the crew were congratulating me, and as usual everyone was put into the Green Room. My mum, dad, brothers and our Sue were still in the auditorium and when the show was over they went to a bar across the road. Meanwhile, I went upstairs to change in my dressing room. At this point I had a moment to myself, and I remember taking a deep breath in, saying 'Fuck me!' and thinking, 'I'm glad that's over.' It felt like a great weight had been lifted off my shoulders. Having calmed myself down, I came out of my dressing room and the producers were in the hall way. Siobhan Green, known to everyone as 'Shu' said, "You were absolutely fantastic Ray! Your performance was absolutely astounding, and we are all very proud of you. Did you enjoy it?" Shu has remained a dear friend to this day.

The other producer that was with her then asked me, "Have you seen Simon?"

"I saw him on set earlier," I said. "Why?"

"Go and see Simon!"

As I walked down the stairs I bumped into Louis Walsh, who said, "Great Job, Ray! Great job!" I felt like I'd been saying "thank you" all evening. I walked towards Simon's dressing room and asked his makeup artist, who was outside his door, "Where's Simon?"

She pointed to the door. "But Leona is in there," she said. "Best wait until she comes out."

I stood in the corridor outside the room and listened to the camaraderie inside. Leona and her family were in there with Simon, and I heard champagne being popped and glasses clinking. A short while after Leona came out of the room. She said, "Ahh, Ray!" then gave me a hug and added, "Well done!" before she and her family moved off down the corridor, heading for the bar.

Simon was stood at his door, "Can I have a chat with you, Ray."

I followed him into his dressing room and stood there with Yvie and a few other people who were already in the room; some of them were from the production team. "Congratulations, Ray!" said Simon. "You've done a great job – you've done me proud. I told you on stage I would give you a career, and right there on the table is your contract with Syco, my record label. Over the next three months you'll be flown to LA, where you will record a Big Band Swing album at Capital Studios. When you get back you have a thirty-gig tour booked – the tickets are already on sale now."

I couldn't believe it! I felt all weak – I just didn't know what to say. I was so relieved that my journey was not over.

"Really!" I replied lamely.

He smiled. "Yes, really Ray!"

I called my mum and dad, telling them they had to come and see me: I had something important to tell them. Then I went back over to Simon and hugged him. I could still hardly believe he had given me an opportunity like this. When he left the room my parents were outside and Simon asked, "Is this Mum?" My mum nodded. "Well, the boy done good. Merry Christmas!" and with that he shook my dad's hand and walked off.

After that we were asked if we'd like to join Sharon Osbourne in her dressing room. There was a lot of champagne and wine, and my mum was tucking into the cheese board. When I told them what Simon had said, the family were all screaming with excitement and the champagne corks popped!

Chapter 9

Post X-Factor

After the show I had to do a day of press conferences and TV appearances, and then I was back up to Liverpool with Mum and Dad to spend Christmas. My new tour manager came up for a day to meet our Sue and to explain what was going to happen with the new tour. There was a lot of press attention in Liverpool and I did a couple of gigs. I remember one gig where I was asked to do an encore but didn't have a song to sing, and there was no time slot for me to do any more. This was my first experience of a backlash from the public and the press. At the time my manager told me not to worry about it, but it did affect me because it was out of my hands and the last thing I wanted was to disappoint my home crowd.

I remember we went to our old village pub, the Caledonian, Ashton. It was a family affair and once again I was behind the bar serving drinks to everyone but not myself drinking because of my singing; alcohol affects my voice and my diary was now solid. It was great to be with the family and have a normal night out. We all had a laugh and a joke as if nothing had happened, and it was great.

When I went back to London I was put up in a really nice swanky hotel in Chelsea. It was one of those proper posh ones with a man at the entrance to open car doors and open the door to the hotel. There were people to take your bags, a concierge, and I had everything I could wish for. This was the life! I was 18 and living it large.

***

I was now with Modest Management and my manager was Georgie Gibbon, who was nice enough and seemed pleasant. My tour manager was Caroline and I knew her as 'the little Rottweiler'; she was a tough cookie but she had a soft spot for me and we would have a good laugh together. About a week after the X Factor I went with the management team I was assigned to and signed a record deal with Sony. I don't remember having anyone look at the contract for me, this was Syco, and so what could be wrong with any contract they put in front of me! This was Simon Cowell, the guy off the telly.

During the first week I was introduced to accountants and lawyers, and this was when it dawned on me that I was in something big. I was only 18 and this was stuff I had never had to deal with in the past. I had no idea what anyone was talking about, I just went with the flow and agreed to everything. There were people around me explaining everything, but anything to do with numbers and accounts went over my head.

It was at this time I was told about the album and what was to be in it. I had no song choice: they told me the songs I was to sing. The whole thing was presented to me prearranged, but I was happy and went along with it. I was then taken to a plush Saville Row tailor, Richard Anderson, to attend a photo shoot. These suits were about £4k each but at the time I didn't realise I was paying for all this out of my record budget as part of my contract. I thought everything was for free. I was enjoying being treated like Royalty. I even had a stylist with me who took me shopping; she was called Faye Sawyer and was lovely down to earth girl. I was picking expensive shoes and coats and it was all put on a debit card, which I thought was sound and I kept saying thank you. She told me it was ok, as it was all being billed to the record label. In other words, I was saying thank you to myself and not knowing it!

That week I was doing a load of press and I was on TV chat shows. I had been on the news before and local TV for the dancing and Brookside, but this was full on. This was all main-stream TV programmes now: I was in the thick of it, where I'd always wanted to be, where I'd dreamed of being - right in the public eye. It was full on and I had to go for media training lessons; these sessions would be for a few hours and would cost £500 a time, but I was advised by my management that I needed the training. They asked if it was ok for them to book me in and I agreed on the back of their advice. Again I was booking the lessons at my own expense, as I was paying for all this out of my budget.

The week was tiring and I was not used to it. I would sleep like a baby and they always had problems waking me up in the morning. Caroline had to have a spare key to my room to make sure I got up. With everything going on I was starting to feel drained and wondering to myself during training sessions and briefings, 'when does the fun stuff start?' It was hard work. I never dreamt that it would be like this, but after only a few weeks the sparkle of TV appearances and media interviews was already beginning to dull.

A week or so later I was at Heathrow with Caroline, booked to go to LA in Economy. When we went to Check-in Caroline asked the well made up girl on the Virgin counter if we could be upgraded. She said she couldn't do anything, but if we went up to the business lounge they may be able to help. When we got there Caroline asked if we could be upgraded. "This is Ray from the X Factor," she explained, "and we're flying to LA to record his new album."

"Yes, I know him", said this older lady, giving me a beaming smile. "Wait here and I'll see what I can do." Caroline turned to me. "If you don't ask, you don't get!"

When the lady came back to us and said, "Yes, we can upgrade you to Business Class." I told her, "Thank you so much!"

So off we flew to LA in Business Class. I wasn't really interested in drinking on the flight, but it was a world above travelling in economy. When you arrived on the plane they offered you a glass of champagne or orange juice. You got a massive seat - and it would go all the way back and turn into a bed. You were given blankets and a pillow, and if you wanted to you could sleep for the nine hour flight as if you were in bed at home. You also got a choice of films. Instead of having to watch the films on a set programme, you got to choose what you watched, and when. When the in-flight meal came round it was a three course affair, you were offered a choice and it was served with proper cutlery. This was definitely the life! The one thing about business class that sticks out for me is that if you press the buzzer, you can get whatever you like to drink. You don't have to wait until *they* decide when you're going to drink or not drink.

When we arrived in LA the whole experience was overwhelming. Here I was in America, and I was a singer with a record deal! We picked up a hire car, which was a Cadillac and it was really nice. Caroline drove and I just stared out the window not believing I was here about to record an album. We drove straight to a luxurious hotel and I was now in such a different world that I sat in my room for a bit thinking, this is amazing! If this is the way my life is going to be, I'm well happy. I phoned my mum to tell her I'd arrived safely and after that because I was so tired from travelling I ordered Room Service. Caroline came into my room and then we went through my diary and what the programme was for LA. After that I just put my head down and slept.

The next day we went to LA Studios where I was introduced to my producer Nigel Wright and musical engineer Richard. Yvie was there too. The studios were like those you see on the TV, with a large desk that recorded each channel, and a recording booth. This was going to be my work space for the next few weeks. When I signed my contracts with Sony I asked if I could have Yvie with me because we got on so well and she could help me get the best out of my voice. We went through certain sound effects they wanted to use, the set list, and what songs we were going to record first. They then started putting some tracks together for me to sing to, and on the first couple of days I laid some vocals down.

When I wasn't needed in the studio I went shopping and touring about with Caroline. We did the tourist thing around LA - went to the beaches, went to the Hollywood sign, did a tour around the stars' houses - and I tried as many American foods as I could think of from seeing them on the TV. Everything in America is big: big roads, big cars, big houses, big food, and big people. I loved it.

On one occasion I remember I had a photo shoot for an LA Magazine, and as I had been in the studio all the time and not got much sun, I got a spray tan to look healthier. The people from the magazine made me smile and we all had a laugh about our accents. They had never heard a strong Liverpudlian accent and I hadn't heard their really nasally American accent. For people speaking the same language we certainly can talk different!

On one of our trips I bought a Breitling watch. It cost £4k and as I had no money on me, Caroline paid for it; she said to pay her back when I got my advance. From then on there was no way I could be parted from this watch. The producer Nigel told me one day in the studio when I was not concentrating on what I was doing and being a bit of dick, if I didn't get it right he would take my watch off me! I still have that watch: it needs a service, and probably the strap looked at, but it is still a prized possession.

The highlight of the trip was when I spent a day in

Capital Studios where all the big acts like Frank Sinatra had recorded. I had a 62 piece band in the studio with me. It just looked amazing to have all those guys in the room - I wish I had taken a photo of it. I felt like one of the greats.

One of the guys in the band, who was about 80, had played with all the greats. As a young man he had played as a solo saxophonist with Frank Sinatra and it was great listening to his stories of these famous artists. I remember one story he told me about when there was a band booked in to record with Frank Sinatra and Frank was about four hours late. When he finally made an appearance he didn't say a thing to anyone - just walked into the recording booth. The conductor struck up the band and they were quarter the way through the first song when Ava Gardiner walked into the studio in a fur coat down to her ankles and high heels. She walked into the booth, whispered something into Frank's ear and then left the studio. The band came to an abrupt stop as Frank took off his headphones and then came out of the booth. He turned to the band and said, 'Fellas, same time tomorrow! You'll be paid double for your time today.' And with that he left the studio. The whole place was completely silent - all they could hear was Ava's heels clicking along the corridor as they both left.

I asked him, "I wonder what she said to him?"

"Son," he said, "Use your imagination!" At this all the band cracked up. All 80 of them…

Simon Cowell visited the Capital Studio while I was recording. He stayed for a couple of hours, and I was happy to see him. He gave me some direction through my headphones while I was in the booth and I thought it was great he had made the effort to come and see me. He had time to have a quick chat with me in a break, asking me if I was enjoying it, which I told him I was. I thanked him for the opportunity, to which he said, "You deserve it Ray and I'm proud of you." Then he added, "I tell you something Ray, you've got some balls doing this at your age. I admire that."

We went back into the studio and he watched me for a little longer and then he left with a goodbye and good luck.

One day I was invited to Sharon Osbourne's house for lunch - the one that was on 'the Osbournes' on the TV. I got to meet Ozzy, Jack, all the dogs. It was insane! Ozzy is a legend and he showed me his pictures he had painted. Sharon asked me what I wanted to eat, as the chef could cook me anything. She asked me what meat I liked, and I told her lamb. "Alright, cool! How about some lamb chops and potatoes - maybe a little bit of veg and some gravy?"

"Yeah, I love gravy!" So their chef cooked me up this gorgeous meal of lamb chops and potatoes.

The house was stunning and all customised, and she must have had about 20 dogs. It was a great afternoon - I just couldn't believe how my life was turning out. Once the album was completed and the studio was happy with the recordings we flew back to London.

***

Once back in London I went back to the hotel in Chelsea again. Caroline used to come into my suite and be like, "Right this is your schedule for today!"

and I would do like, 12 interviews a day back to back and my brain was just fried saying the same thing to different people. I tried to make each one slightly different, but obviously they all ask the same questions - the same thing day in day out. It was all very exciting but generally trying, and I remember my mum seeing me one time and she said "Son, I saw you on TV and you looked shattered. Are you alright?"

"Yeah, Mum! I'm shattered but I'm alright. I'm doing all kinds of things."

My mum saw a difference in me, though. I had put a bit of weight on as well, cos I was just eating all the really nice stuff. I was not dancing as much, and was not exercising; I was on the phone or I was in interviews and I could feel the change in myself. All the exciting stuff had sort of finished and things were becoming routine. If anything it was becoming a bit of a drag. I missing home too; I was only a young kid then, and this was the first time I had really been away from family. I didn't really know how to look after myself, so I ate what I wanted and drank what I wanted. In no way was I doing myself any favours and no one was around me giving me advice on diet and how to look after myself. Looking back, maybe I should have been a bit more adult, but I'd never had to grow up: I'd always had my mum and dad looking after me.

The X Factor Tour began on 17th February 2007. There were 12 dates around the country and they had sold 100,000 tickets in the first week of sales. The first venue was in Newcastle and on the tour were the top eight live finalists of X Factor. We all received payments for the tour: Leona got the most for being the winner, and I was paid the second highest fee. Caroline blagged me a free BMW, including insurance. She had rung them and said Ray wants a BMW, and this lovely chap Johnathan Clark, who I'm still friends with today and have since bought several cars from, supplied the BMW 1 Series - all I had to do was put the petrol in it. It was all part of a sponsorship deal: the Series 1 was a new model for BMW and they just wanted me to be seen in it to help sales. Luckily it worked too, as BMW sold more Series 1 that quarter after I was pictured picking up my brand new car. That car was the nuts. It was all black with a leather and Alcantara interior and it was the first brand spanking new car I had ever had. I was driving it around like I was the bee's knees - racing away from the lights and driving it everywhere I could. The best moment was when I was at a set of lights when one of the lads that used to give me a bit of stick at school pulled up in a bit of a tatty Ford. I lowered the window electronically while he wound down the window manually, gave it large and burned away from the lights. 'Cock.'

The tour was fun and the experience of playing in front of full crowds up and down the country was great. We were all a bit young to be rock'n'roll, so there were no real antics on tour. We were left to our own devices though, so it wasn't like when we were in the house. Eton Road was on the tour as well, but again we weren't on social terms. Fair enough, it must have been hard for them, as I now had a solo record deal and an album about to be released. Louis Walsh popped into one of the gigs to have a talk with Eton Road, but it seems nothing came of this.

We were playing to excited crowds of thousands of all ages, not only the tiny tot kids who were the big fans of the show, but also their mums and dads who brought them. There were also the teenagers who were at their first ever gig. It was electric and back stage we used to listen to who got the biggest cheer. It was always a judgement call between me and Leona. I had a set with dancing and singing and put on the best show I could every night. I used all my dancing skills in my act and would bounce around the whole stage with my backing dancers. I used to come off the set soaked in sweat and full of energy. This was what it was all about, and I loved it.

The fans for the show got everywhere. There would always be a big crowd at the stage door after the show, and I would be there signing autographs for youngsters and then having a picture taken with Mum and Dad. On top of that, the fans would always manage to find what hotel we were staying in and would be hanging about all day. Wherever we went though, I was happy to sign autographs, as these were the fans that put me where I was on the 'X-Factor'. I remember one evening Leona just blanked everyone waiting to see us all and jumped on the bus. I thought to myself, 'I would never do that - it would make me feel so bad.' But I think she'd may have just had a bad day.

None of the judges came to any of the gigs, and after I finished the tour that was my commitment to X Factor over. The album 'Doing it My Way' was released on Mother's Day, 12th March 2007 and reached number one in the album charts, going Platinum in the first week of release. I was given £75,000 advance when the album was released, and one of the first things I did was pay back Caroline for that watch!

Between the album release and the tour I was on a high. I was gigging all over the place, all over the world actually. It was non-stop, but some gigs at the time stand out. I was asked to do a private show in Egypt for an Egyptian Prince, getting paid a lot of money for just the one night. Then I was invited to Dubai to do a gig for a very wealthy businessman's daughter, who was thirteen at the time. She had seen me in the American magazine I did the photo-shoot for when I was recording my album in the US. I was doing what I always dreamt I would be doing, touring the world and performing. Everything was great and I was living the dream.

One day they told me they needed to get me an agent, on the grounds that they could only do the music side, and I now needed a theatre agent. I agreed that I'd love to do West End, and so myself and Gregory met with a few people, including Peter Brooks of the CAM Management Team. We went down to see them in their gorgeous offices in middle of Piccadilly - very, very posh. OH, WOW! A top agency, I thought. What a dream! Yeah, this is great; I like this.

***

I was still living with my mum and dad - flitting in and out. Kirsty, my girlfriend, was getting annoyed and started suggesting that we get our own place and that we deserved it. She was fuelling me to get out of my mum and dad's, driving a wedge between us, almost controlling me. I guess I just went along with it all – as I usually do – and we went and had a look at a couple of houses. Then, quick as that, we bought one and I got a mortgage on the First Time Buyer scheme. It was a brand new, four-bedroom town house in Cheshire. There was a rain shelter over the front door and a garden all landscaped and patioed, with blue up-lifter lights. It was carpeted throughout, and we chose the bathroom and had a kitchen kitted out with coffee machines and a fantastic American style fridge. Everything was high spec - gorgeous wooden floors; 55 inch TV in the wall and a mini-gym; my own en-suite, two living rooms, spare room and a double bathroom; Juliet balcony - it was a real show biz house, and I was just 19.

I was wrapped up in the relationship with Kirsty at the time. That was the only kind of life I ever knew: I have always had a girl-friend or a partner alongside me because of the dancing. I wasn't thinking of marriage - we just were seeing 'how it goes'. She was the instigator of a lot of things. I never really made any of the decisions, just went along with everything to keep the peace. This was me - the people pleaser.

***

The album tour started in the September of 2007 and it was a 30 date run, including Liverpool that sold out twice and where I ended up doing three nights. Prior to the start of the tour I was asked what I wanted on set. Did I want dancers? Did I want a band? What sort of light show, pyrotechnics did I want? Again, little did I know that all this would be coming out of my tour budget – that in fact I was paying for it all. If I *had* known, I would've just settled for a microphone and star cloth on the back of the stage, but I didn't know this at the time and went for a big glitzy show. There was a tour budget and it was explained to me by my management, but I just spent it because I thought that was how a tour went.

Kirsty suggested I should have dancers and that she could be one of them, so this way she would be on tour with me, which at the time seemed like a good idea. My management agreed with it, but they did say I would need a choreographer. With a band, dancers, choreographer and a large set, this tour was getting expensive, but I was oblivious to the business side of what I was doing. I was just acting like a big banana superstar, giving my bird and her mate a job. There was a merchandising desk set up for each gig with the usual paraphernalia of T-shirts, mugs, programmes, buttons, key rings and posters. These did really well and I got a cut of the profits.

The first venue was at the Rhyll Pavilion in North Wales on the 26th September, 2007. It was a sell-out. It went really well and it felt great to be on tour with my own show; I even had two support acts 'Laura Critchley' and 'Lauren Rose'. I didn't really get to know them, though, as I was shadowed by Kirsty on this tour. She was very possessive and didn't like me speaking to other girls, even if they were fellow artists on the same show. The most memorable nights were in Liverpool, where I was well received and where it was great playing to my home crowd. The nights were ecstatic, with people standing up, dancing in the aisles and screaming out my name. I felt like a star. It was great. The local press reported that the show was 'a Home-coming Spectacular, with style and panache.' What could go wrong!

***

When Kirsty and I used to go out to dinner together, or out and about, people really started to recognise me, especially in Liverpool. Once I even had someone take my fork away from my mouth as I was about to eat, and ask me for a picture. A bit bizarre, and it annoyed me a little, cos there *is* a way to introduce yourself, but I guess everyone is different! This type of thing would really grate on Kirsty and she would say, "You can't do that!" and I would say, "Nah! – it's sound". I would rather shrug it off and not make a scene because I would hate, at the time, for people to think I was rude, I wanted to be known as a nice guy. I was always self-conscious about what people thought of me, and also I didn't want to upset my management, as they would be the first to tell me off if I was caught doing anything wrong. I always was aware of what people thought. That's just the way I was brought up. Even today my dad still says to me, 'Be nice to the people on the way up, as you will see them again on the way down. Don't have anyone talking about you.'

Kirsty wasn't always like this but at times, depending on her mood, she could be quite sharp with people. On some occasions when a fan asked her to take a picture she'd say, no – no way! So I'd say to the fan, "Ok – get your mate to take it then." Some people could be awkward and pushy, which I understand from her point of view, but this was something I'd already accepted. I was now in the public arena and with this I had to accept that the public wanted a part of me. Many had spent their hard-earned cash voting for me or buying my album, so signing an autograph or having my picture taken with them was a small price for me to pay. Great advice from my dad was a quote from Elvis Presley. 'The day I stop signing autographs is the day I stop performing.'

***

Kirsty and I took luxury holidays in places like Greece and Tenerife, Jamaica and Dubai. We had a great good time: we swam with dolphins, stayed in Five Star hotels and flew everywhere Business Class. I thought living the high life was going to last forever. Of course, by now the money was starting to dwindle away but I thought, that's all right, cos I'll have another album out soon and another payment.

The day came when I finally got a meeting with Sony again. I was so happy that things seemed to be getting back on the move, and I recall going upstairs to the office of Syco, Simon Cowell's label. Tim Byrne, his right hand man at the time, was there to represent him. Back then only about 12 to 15 people used to work in the offices. Looking around, there were golden and platinum discs on the walls; it was very glamorous and I thought, 'How exciting is this – and I'm a part of it!' One of the receptionists asked me if I wanted a tea or coffee, and then we sat in Reception drinking tea until we were told they were ready to see us.

Sonny's office was really plush, like those you see on the TV. There was a desk with executive toys on it, a sideboard with ornaments, and walls dressed with framed albums, gold platinum you name it they were on the wall. The man behind the desk greeted me with, "Congratulations on getting your first album going platinum!" He shook my hand and we sat down to a bit of an awkward silence after some small chat of how have you been? Has it been enjoyable? Simon sends his love – he's sorry he can't be here today, but he's in LA working. He then asked, "So what do you want to do for your next album?"

'What? I don't know! You were in control last time, so just do the same again please!' was what I thought in my head. What came out was, "What do I want to do? Well, I guess something along similar lines." I remember trying to make something up to sound like I knew what I was talking about, and after a few words I thought I was re-pitching myself as if it was day one again.

Noticing my panic Georgie and Richard, my management, interrupted and spoke up for me. "Well, we can see Ray going down a presenter route - keeping him young, taking his jazz background a little more contemporary into songs with a bit more of an upbeat tempo."

At which Sonny paused and then asked, "Do you write music, Ray? Do you play any instruments?"

"No, but I'm a quick learner," I said a bit desperately, "I can certainly learn if that's what you want!"

All of a sudden from being one of their platinum selling artists, I'd become somebody that couldn't do anything except sing. They knew now that I couldn't play an instrument, and they were aware that I wasn't a writer: I was only a singer, and I'd gone from being this guy that was doing pretty well to God knows what. "OK! Well, we'll have to get together and think up some ideas. We'll get you back in next week and have a brain storm."

It was like going through the audition process all over again. Well, that was a waste of time, I thought, so I left the room after an hour or so, and I went home and waited impatiently. From the time I woke up to the time I went to bed I was in deep thought; I turned everything over and over in my mind until my head was in a spin. I was starting to think things like, 'Surely they won't let me go! I've got a platinum selling album; I've got some credence there. *And* I've had a sell-out tour. I haven't upset anyone; I've done everything asked of me, and to a decent standard.' So in my head I was convinced I would be sound. Then my manager sent me an email that just said, "Let's catch up."

I phoned the office right away, and Georgie answered. "Hi Ray! Richard wants to chat with you – is it alright now, or do you want me to call you later?"

"No, I'm fine to talk now. I'm not doing anything am I?" I giggled nervously, and she passed me over to Richard Griffiths.

"Hi Ray! How you doing? Everything OK? Are you keeping well? Look, I hate to tell you over the phone – I'd much rather you come to the office, but obviously you're in Liverpool, so I have no other choice, as I didn't want to delay telling you. I've just got off the phone to Syco and they're basically not going to continue with you as of today."

There was a long pause before I answered. "Wow!

Really....!" I stayed silent for a while and then thought about my reaction. I could either get all upset and emotional or stay positive. I stayed positive. "Right, Ok, that's fine obviously. I've had an amazing time, it's just sad that it's all over."

"Yes...well, you know Ray," he went on, "they just said they couldn't see what the next stage was for you." Then he added, "Look I have to go to a meeting now, but I think you're up in London next week for an audition. Pop into the office and I'll explain more then." With that he hung up.

I stood staring out of the kitchen window: my first thought was, 'Lucky I still have money in the bank!' but on the other hand I was in complete and utter panic mode and devastated to say the least. 'What next?'

Kirsty walked into the kitchen and saw me looking out of the window in a daze. She asked, "What's up?"

"I've had some bad news." I took a deep breath. "I've just been dropped from the label." As I said this the reality hit that little bit harder and I burst into tears. This was the moment I'd always been afraid of, and there I was - my world had come crashing down on me in a year. All the hard work just washed away with one phone call.

"What the fuck! ...why?"

"I have to go and see Richard next week when I'm in London and he has more time, but the short of it is that they didn't know what to do with me, or what direction to take me."

She just hugged me as I sobbed on her shoulder.

***

That night I lay in bed and just stared at the ceiling thinking about what had just happened and what this last year was all about. My brain was working over-time, and I began to get angry and think of things cyn-ically. Was I just part of a machine that churned out aspiring singers year after year? Back at the start it had felt different because I respected the platform I was given to launch my career, but looking back now.... the three application forms arriving a few days apart, even though I failed to fill the first one in. The man in the stadium that my dad spotted watching me before he even arrived at my row. Them telling me that they knew about Brookside and not to mention it. The fact I had a contract with Mrs Byatt but it finished on my 18th Birthday. The fact Eton Road got the finals, and we had been to the same drama school and I had audi-tioned for the same band.

I had fluffed my song in Boot Camp but got a second chance. I didn't smash my song at the Judges' House either, and then I was saved by Simon Cowell during the show for the second time. Ben Mills was out of the show just before me because he had complained about the final song choice not being true to him. Vocally he was a better singer than me. The final song choice was arguably more geared for Leona, but I was told I already had a contract before the final was over, and the gigs had already been planned. Now a year on the runners-up were popping off the end of the conveyer belt. That was me finished with Syco. I looked at where I was now, and I had a Number One Platinum Album under my belt, a house, a bit of money in the bank and prospects - so not all was bad I suppose.

On the face of it though, my whole world had crashed around me. I had no further contracts and just had to rely on my managers Richard and Georgie and my agents at CAM (Creative Artist Management). If I'm honest, I did go into a downer. Nothing happening for months, I lost the determination and drive; I got really tubby and lethargic and felt like it had all been just a waste. I had £40k in the bank at the time when they dropped me in 2007. I'd spent a lot of money on cars, holidays, watches and clothes, anything I wanted. I thought there was going be no end to this: I had a Number One Platinum Album, I was signed to Syco and I was only 19 - why would I think it would end!

Here it is! Me number "Thirty thousand and ten – Don't forget that number – I'm Ray Quinn!" Me very words from the X Factor, little did I know how quickly me decision to audition would change me life!

All me family and friends supporting me during the X Factor. I remember our Robin on the telly said "Made-up you're doing well, cos if you make it, I can have all your old clothes and my room back!"

Dad, Simon Cowell and me mum back stage at the X Factor. Me dad said "Sound him in'he!"

Me auntie Sue and me mum back stage at the X Factor – week one. Mum was fuming that they dressed me in a waistcoat and T-Shirt! "I could have dressed you better! She said

The X Factor voting begins! The good old days of 'Myspace' me uncle Ste set up to help get votes and the one of the left was stuck up all around Liverpool

X Factor with the lovely Kate Thornton

A little cuddle with me nan at home

The very talented Melanie Hill came to show her support backstage – X Factor

Me and me guy-liver! Robin, Darren mum and dad backstage at the X Factor – why I'm caked in makeup I don't know!

Party celebrations at our house after coming second on the X Factor with me man and me mum – drinks all round! Note the little token American balloon – purely cos me mum knew I was going to LA – it's the little things, she never misses a trick!

Dancing on Ice show – this good looking lunch turned up to give their support! X

Me mum looking stunning and me dad scrubbing up nicely for the opening night when I played 'Doody' in Grease 2008

Me proud parents showing off me brick outside the Cavern in Liverpool. It has been de-faced a few times! But it's still there!

Back stage at Grease the musical. As you can see it took me a while to perfect the quiff! I don't know why – but I don't look too happy in this picture!

Me young mother and glowing dad coming to see me as 'Danny Zuko' and Emma as 'Sandy' in Grease on the opening night

Dancing on Ice again! With me poor nan who wasn't very well at the time but she was determined to show her support and never once let me down

Absolutely Buzzing! And slightly smug! I'm the winner of 'Dancing on Ice'

This is Yvie my vocal coach on the X Factor. She came to LA with me and we spent some good times together, I will always have a soft spot for her

Pissed!

My 21st Birthday 007 style – personalised drinks menu for the night! I drank me-self sober! Me Uncle Phil had far too many and was sick at the back of the garden – which Bruno (my puppy Jack Russell) helped himself to the following morning!

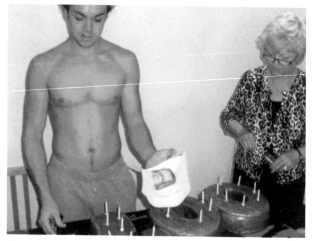

Hungover….. Cake for breaky!

Party time with me and me gorgeous Emma
My 21st Birthday Bash

My 21st Birthday Bash
Darren, Dad, Me, Robin – lads looking dapper! Plus me dad's little belly! Love him

(Top) Me Harley me dream bike! (Right) Suzuki mu current toy! (Left) Parked in me lounge for safety (typical Scouser) (Middle bottom) Me first bike aged 20!... fell of that one a few times!! (Middle top) Harley 48 I only had it three months, we move house and I had nowhere to put it!

Me and me beautiful wife

Working hard in the gym – but always time for a cheeky selfie!

In the gym again! - I guess I don't need to explain why!

Daddy time

I love this picture with my little man Harry

Tatted and Twatted

Little Harry is was so tiny and fragile

Me, little Harry and Emma on our holidays, Harry still getting used to what a camera is! But he will learn from the best, Dads not shy of a camera or two!

More Daddy time with my handsome chappy x

Back in the studio. Good times!

My manager Steve Coxshall and me popping the champers! After signing contracts for the EP - New York here we come!

At the Cavern in Liverpool backstage with all me mates showing love 2014

Chapter 10

Post Syco

My management team were still looking after me, and I never complained: I sent them Christmas cards and used to pop down to say hello. That's how I'd been brought up; always be nice to people.

It took me over six months to get my next contract - the part of Doody in Grease in the West End. When I got the part, I just couldn't believe it after being out of work for all that time. I'd been playing small gigs as Ray Quinn off the X-Factor, which was not the heights of where I wanted to be, but it paid some of the bills. I remember doing three auditions for Grease; after each audition I hoped I'd got the part and then finally Peter Brook of CAM phoned me to tell me I had and I was ecstatic. When I found out I celebrated with Kirsty with a Chinese takeaway and a bottle of cider. Kirsty was pleased for me but not over the moon. I'd been given a six month contract, and even though I promised I'd be home on Sundays, she knew I was going to be based in London for long periods of time.

It paid £3,500 per week and so I moved to London for that. I had to pay my management and my agency and my digs out of what I got - 30% to the agency etc. plus my tax on top and £1500 per month rent – but I never lifted a hand or finger to do anything ; my management team did it all for me. My tax was taken out and they paid the accountant all the money monthly.

Looking back, I suppose someone should have been advising me of company tax stuff and so on, but to tell you the truth I just wasn't interested. All I wanted to know was what I'd got left once everything was paid. The accountant said, "I'm no financial advisor - I can't tell you how to spend your money," but I was paying myself all of £4K a month, so maybe he should have been smarter than that.

***

While I was rehearsing I moved to Radlett to stay with Caroline and her boyfriend; she took me in for few weeks at £50 per week toward my dinner. I felt awkward cos they would argue sometimes. He was a property developer and they'd met when she bought a house in one of his developments. I felt like I was in the way a bit, so I asked Georgie find me a property, explaining that I didn't know what to do, or who to go to. She said to leave it with her, and sent me loads of properties on my Blackberry. One of these was the £1500 a month flat in Clapham, which I took as soon as I saw it.

It was a proper bachelor flat, in a terrace overlooking the railway and with a living room under a big glass roof: it was great - like a hotel! I filled the freezer up with peas, chicken, potatoes and frozen sausages; Kirsty never cooked anything, so that's all I knew - stuff from the freezer. I never ate fresh fruit and veg;

my life was Coca cola and chocolate! I'd always been on the go in different towns and places, and I'd never learned to take care of myself.

The first time I got to meet the cast of Grease was when we all had to go to Pineapple Studios. When I arrived and went to Reception I asked the receptionist where the cast of Grease was and was really proud to tell her I was part of it. She directed me to the top of the stairs in Studio 7 and when I got there it was to find a seating area full of cast members, dancers and teachers waiting to be ushered into the studio. Apart from me, they all seemed to know one another and I was a bit embarrassed. Being a little shy, I'm not really into crowds and awkward situations, so I moved down the corridor a bit out of the way. I phoned home to pass the time, to distract me from having to speak to anyone.

After a while the cast was called into the room. 'Cast of Grease, please!' I found a corner out of the way and put my bag down, then tried to introduce myself to as many people I could, but I couldn't build up enough courage to speak to this stunning blonde girl that was in the room: my confidence over the last six months had taken a bit of a battering. About ten minutes later David Ian the producer came into the room. "Right, Guys! If you'd like to take a seat, and we can have a quick briefing." He called to the room. We all found a chair and sat in a big circle. "Right! Let's do the traditional thing and introduce ourselves - what your name is, what you're playing - so we can get to know who everyone is."

As people introduced themselves I couldn't keep my eyes off the blonde girl with her curly hair and lovely red lips. She was wearing a white blouse, skinny jeans and a pair of little high heels. She said, "Hi! I'm Emma and I play Marty."

To which David Ian cheekily remarked. "Of course you do!" and the whole room laughed nervously.

When it came round to my turn to introduce myself I looked around the room to see if anyone recognised me and said, "Hi! I'm Ray Quinn and I'm playing Doody." This was just like drama class back at Mrs Byatt's!

Rehearsals took three weeks, and then it was my first live show in the West End. By now my confidence had been rising, and I felt part of something again. The first night was a full house. I loved the part of Doody; it's a great role to play, and I think he has the best song of the show. Everyone was there to have fun, with the audience dancing in the aisles and hen dos in every night. People were there just to have a great time and it was all really infectious.

I did eight shows a week, and it was good to have a regular wage again. It was at this time that I moved into the flat in Clapham. For the first couple of months I would try to get home to Liverpool, but it was too much for me. It would be a 5 hour drive there and a 5 hour drive back; the train wasn't much easier and wasn't reliable anyway, as they always seemed to be doing engineering works at the weekends. I also tend to drive a bit fast and this brought me to the attention of the police a couple of times. I wasn't enjoying going back to Liverpool at the time either, though I did like seeing my mum and dad and our Sue. Kirsty wasn't really bothered, and although I kept in regular contact with her by phone, as time went on I felt like we were drifting apart. I liked having my own space too. I was 19 and living in London with my own flat and a little Audi TT. What can I say - life was good!

I started to get friendlier with the cast from Grease and having a laugh back stage. In my contract it stated that there was a car to take me home after the show. I felt bad if I didn't use it, so at first I didn't go out with the crew. I just stuck to routine, but all the time I was missing out on a 19 year old's life in London. I should have been out enjoying myself, learning about life, becoming a young man.

About four months into the contract I was growing more and more distant from Kirsty. I was getting independent and she was not in control any more: I was growing up. Eventually I phoned her one day and said we needed to talk. Obviously she realised something was wrong and wanted to know immediately, but I wanted to go home at the weekend and speak to her face to face. I remember a lot of people in Grease breaking up their current relationships and going with people in the show: there must have been something in the air. At that time, though, it was just me; I didn't want a relationship, though. I knew I was slowly falling in love with Emma, but I didn't want a relationship. I didn't want to be tied down: I wanted to be in London and be a chap; I wanted a bit of fun.

I realised I was being a bit off with her, and one weekend I went to a christening I'd promised I'd go, even though I didn't really want to be there. I went to the after party and had a bottle of beer. Her mum and dad came over and asked if everything was ok with me. I told them I was sound, but then later I sat down with Kirsty and put my cards on the table. I told her I felt a bit trapped, stuck, and I wanted to move on.

She reacted immediately with, "You don't want to be with me any more?"

"It's not that I don't want to be with you." I heard myself saying, but thinking in my head, no I don't want to be with you.

"I'll move to London with you then."

"No, I don't want you to move to London. I want to be on my own," I managed to be brave enough to tell her that.

Her mum overheard the conversation, realised Kirsty was upset and came storming over. "Kirsty what's wrong? Why are you upset? What have you been saying to her?" she snapped at me.

"It's nothing, Mum - it's fine!"

"It's not fine! What are saying to her? You saying you don't want to be with her, after all that youse have been through together? Who do you think you are?" her mother snarled. She was not the nicest lady at the best of times.

"Pauline," I started to explain. "She asked me what was wrong, and she wanted to talk to me about it. I told her I didn't want to talk about it here, but she insisted I did. Look, I can't be having this! I'm going – alright?" and with that I stood up and made my way to the front door.

"Yeah, alright! Walk off, walk away! Don't think I don't know about the phone calls youse have been having. I swear if you do anything to upset my daughter, there'll be nothing down for ya!" she shouted after me.

With that I got in my car and drove back to London.

When we bought the house, we'd signed with both our names but I had paid for it. Kirsty was working in Blackpool at a Hotel as part of a cabaret act. She earnt a bit of money but not a lot doing this.

Anyway, it was sort of left that day with no conclusion. The next weekend, Kirsty got hysterical and Pauline and Leigh took me upstairs when I went back to the house under Kirsty's request.

"Kirsty wants you to stay with her; she loves you!" Lee explained to me.

I was crying. "It's not want I want," I told them. "I don't want to be in a relationship."

"Kirsty is accusing you of being gay." He raised his eyebrows. "Are you gay?"

"No, of course I'm not Gay! I just don't want to be tied down."

Lee was a really nice guy: he'd never really got involved and now he was being kind, saying he'd always be there for me, whatever. He liked me and was sad that the relationship had to come to this, but he understood that things run their course.

I went back to London and Kirsty phoned me the next day. "Honest to God," I told her, "this has got to stop!"

"I can't believe you've dumped me over the phone, Ray!"

"Look, Kirsty, the last thing I want to do is break your heart. Can't we move on?" I tried to convince her that it was all over and there was no point in calling me, I was not going to change my mind.

She was so angry that I didn't want to be with her any more, and now she really lost it, saying that it was our house, and if I was dumping her, she wanted half. I pointed out that although we'd been living together for two years we weren't engaged. There was no equity in the house, which was mine anyway. There was no question of me kicking her out, but if she could find somewhere else to live, I would look after her financially until she set herself up again. In the meantime I asked her to sign the house officially over to me.

Well, eventually it came to solicitors' letters, and after weeks and weeks she did agree to sign the house over.

I had to return to Liverpool a few weeks later to collect some of my stuff from the house. Kirsty was there, still questioning me about why I was doing this to her. Since I had made the break I was happy to be on my own. While I had been away, Kirsty had let the house go. She had been smoking in it, which she knew I hated and the place was a mess. I was with my brother, our Robin, and we just got my stuff loaded into his van and left.

***

Back in London I started socialising, but not a huge amount, going out in the same group as Emma. Emma had split up with her boyfriend not long before I split with Kirsty, so we were both single and I was getting to know her better. At the end of the night the both of us would be left together; we would share cabs and I would carry her bags, trying hard now to impress her. She was like no other girl I had met before. I was besotted with her.

I bought a new Audi from the Park Lane garage and asked Emma if she wanted to come along and see it with me. Of course, we got papped when I picked the car up. I was so naïve in those days. Of course it was the garage that tipped them off; this was a bit of free advertising for their car and their garage. What the garage didn't bargain for was the story that broke in the papers. They must have thought all their birthdays had come at once. There I was in this new car and with this gorgeous blonde that was Emma. One of the tabloids ran a story on it the very next day, but before they released it my management got wind of it and Georgie phoned me first thing in the morning. I was asked if I was having an affair and I denied it, as I had only just split up with Kirsty and had not even got past first base with Emma. Not for want of trying….

Kirsty phoned me in a real state, wanting to know who Emma was, and accusing me of cheating on her. "You better tell her to watch her back, cos I'm coming down to London to find her! And you know that brand new car you bought, I'm gonna to smash it to pieces!" she yelled - or something like that. It was no good trying to reason with her; she only believed what she wanted to. Her parents went to my parents, and said, "What's wrong with him? Why is he acting like this?" The answer was easy. I was a 21 year old boy who just wanted to have some freedom. I had known Kirsty a long time and been in a relationship with her since I was only 16, but she was like really heavy and full on, with her mother pushing things as well. Anyway, a couple of weeks, a month went by, and she never carried out her threats.

Kirsty sold the story of our relationship to the Star newspaper. Apart from claiming that I'd cheated on her, she never said anything bad about me. She even said I was good in bed, which was a bonus – ha ha! It made me laugh after she'd been so nasty on the phone to me, but she obviously got a bit of money from it. She was on the front cover in her underwear, which wasn't tasteful and didn't make her look good. She was obsessed with Page 3 glamour, so she lapped it all up and took it as a good career opportunity.

Emma and I were getting friendlier all the time. She started staying with me, and I fell deeply in love with her and asked her to move in; it was a mutual thing, (about three months of dating). One day I got a text from her saying, "You probably notice I act weird around you, but it's cos I really like you." Emma! I couldn't believe it, I went in the next day all cocky, and when I told her I'd got the text she said, 'Oh God! I shouldn't have said anything!' After that I was lapping it up all day; I was like the king of the castle - the fittest girl I had ever seen in my life fancied me and I couldn't believe my luck! I must have done her head in after that, cos I felt really smug.

"What you doing tonight?"

"I'm going home."

"I'll drop you off!"

Anyway, this gave me the chance to say about the text again, and to tell her the feeling was mutual. The next time we went out I took her for dinner, and after that we went for nice walks together, or to the cinema or to a pub after the show.

***

My six month contract with Grease was coming to an

end shortly after this, and it was then that Emma and I started seeing each other as a couple and she moved into my flat. She was great to be with - she could even cook and she sorted out my clothes, so I was well looked after again. We were in love and we loved each other's company. Here I was back on top again.

Our colleagues on Grease all loved me and Emma. Still to this day it's the best job I have ever done. Our friends were gorgeous people; it felt like I'd become one of them and I was comfortable, sure that this was what I really should be doing. The show had already been in the West End for God knows how many years; I was there 6 months and Emma had a year. After she moved in a lot of time had gone by and I hadn't been back to my little house for a while. My mum phoned me and asked if I was going to sort the house out, her advice being to rent it. I told her I didn't want to store the furniture, so she suggested meeting me there so we could make some arrangements to let it furnished. I rushed home by car, only to get stopped by the police on the way. I was doing 130mph, and I eventually went to court and got a 28 day ban and £1,500 fine.

I then had to rush back to London leaving Emma with my mum in Liverpool.

My mum phoned Emma and they went to my house only to find that Kirsty had changed the locks, which meant calling in a locksmith to the tune of £280! I've never been back there to this day. When I phoned my mum and Emma from London they said, "Do you want the good news or the bad news? The good news is you won't have to put your stuff into storage because she's taken everything."

It turned out she had in fact taken the couches, PlayStation, jewellery, washer-dryer, beds, curtains, blinds, table and chairs, my gym – the lot! A woman scorned, and I have to laugh. I don't know what she did with it all, but she did me a favour cos at least it was all gone. A lot of money went into that house, but I was happier and it was just furniture. All she left me was a note, a bottle of wine and a pint glass, but now I felt free. My dad cleaned the place up and it has been rented out ever since. I never saw Kirsty again

We were home all over Christmas that year and after that I went to do pantomime in Peterborough. One day I'd got a phone call from my manager asking me if I'd ever done panto. I was on the loo at the time, but when I took the call I was excited. Apparently there were three offers - First Family, Kudos and High Town Productions. The question was, who was paying the most, and it was High Town Productions at £90k. "Bloody hell," I said, "Really! Well what you waiting for! Get off the phone and tell them I'll do it." It was me, Fay Tozer, Brian Capron (Villain of the year 2002) for his portrayal Richard Hillman in Coronation Street. The three of us turned up for Press Day in Peterborough at a massive brand new theatre.

There was already a panto in town around the corner that people usually went to. Here we were, a Corrie star, a Steps star and me, all in a limousine turning up to a theatre with 50ft banners with our faces on them. We were led into a room where we were greeted with champagne, loads of PR and press. The production company was made up of two blokes who told us, "We've been searching for the perfect theatre. We're putting all our money in this," and from then on I felt instinctively that something was wrong. We were told nothing about ticket sales, box office takings - nothing. Anyway, we got stuck into rehearsals, which was a lot of fun. The cast and crew were good fun too, and we all got on well. I was starting to enjoy myself. After a few weeks of rehearsals it eventually came to Opening Night.

"How we doing, Mate?" I asked the producer, "Is the audience in?"

"Well, it's a bit quiet, Mate." He looked embarrassed.

"So how many are in?"

"About 80." He looked worriedly at the floor.

"And how many does the theatre hold?"

"Seven hundred."

"Are you having a laugh?" I didn't know what to think, this was a first for me. "Well I suppose we have to get on with it." And we did the show.

The poor guy - Gary Nicholson I think his name was - who played the genie had to paint his whole body blue every day twice a day, and we were playing to no more than100 people for the first week. At the end of that week we looked at our bank accounts and not one of us had been paid.

"When are we getting paid, Mate?"

"Well, I'd like to buy you a glass of wine in the foyer and have a chat."

We all sat in the lobby, and the guy who was the producer, director and also played the dame told us he'd spent a lot of money on the production, his life savings; he and his partner in the panto had spent close to £100k on costumes alone.

He looked anxiously at the cast collected in the bar and then said, "Have whatever you want, I'm buying! Would you like some food?"

When we told him we just wanted to know what was going on, he admitted that the box office wasn't picking up, but he was expecting 300 to 400 Xmas Eve evening, so he might be able to pay us a little something out of that. There was no way, though, that we would be getting our full wages! Meanwhile, I was paying for a luxury apartment right next door to the theatre, with car parking at £700 per week, cos I'd thought I'd be able to afford it. He reckoned that the best he could do was pay rehearsal fees up to date, but for the rest of the run no wages. £5k for rehearsals, when I'd been promised £90k!

Luckily for me, I had a received a call from Georgie during rehearsals to tell me I'd been selected to appear on ITV Dancing on Ice in January, and I was already going to the local skating rink to practice.

The director/producer was crying now. "I've put all my money into this! I don't know what to do, but I would really appreciate it if you could see this through with me and just keep this show going - it's my dream!"

I felt sorry for him, but this was a big ask, it was not as if I had money to burn, and I was not going to pay to be in someone else's dream. This was very surreal. I had been promised a lot and looking at not receiving much at all compared to the work load.

"Well, look," I told him, "I think I'm quite a nice person, and I'm all up for doing favours, but not working for free: I can't afford to."

After the meeting I got on the phone to Georgie. "I'm

working hard towards Dancing on Ice, and you need to get me paid up to date and get me out of this contract."

Georgie was fine with it. She understood and said she would call the producer right away and get it all sorted. I was just walking out of the room after making the call when I bumped into the producer, who was having a cigarette outside. He looked drained, the troubles of the world on his shoulders.

"How's it going Ray?" he asked, and then added, "Sorry about all this! I hope you stay with the production. I have the utmost respect for you - you are such a talent."

I smiled at him, but his phone started ringing in his pocket before I could answer. He looked at the screen and then looked at me, rolling his eyes. "It's your manager..."

I coughed loudly, in a feeble attempt to try and warn Georgie that I was standing there with the producer, but I don't think she heard me. I watched as he mumbled, "Yes... I understand....Yes..... I agree... and I must apologise.... Yes..." He finished with. "I will have Ray's money in his account first thing in the morning."

He then turned and looked at me, rolled his eyes again and took a long drag of his cigarette. That night I went back to the flat next to the theatre, packed my bags and left.

It goes without saying that they were in breach of contract by not paying me, but I was the only one that walked, the others stayed. Faye Tozer was pregnant at the time but carried on to the end. The other producer ran off to Australia and was never seen again. The theatre went off the rails and it was rumoured that it was down to the terrific amount of money lost because of the pantomime. A while later I met up with Gary the genie, and I said wasn't it a nightmare! He told me I didn't know the worst of it; it had all gone downhill faster than a car without breaks – one night only 10 people turned out! Gary reckoned that it hadn't been advertised properly and that being just outside town, the theatre wasn't really in a good position. He also told me that the building burnt down, the rumour being that the guy that owned it, Renato Fusicol, set it on fire and tried to claim on the insurance to get back the money he'd lost. The insurance company named him, though, and he was done for fraud.

***

Man Jailed for Peterborough Broadway Theatre Fraud

4 August 2014 Last updated at 21:25 BST

A man has been jailed for three years and three months after the theatre company he was running lost £1m while he was already disqualified as a company director.
Paul Coxwell's company reopened the Broadway Theatre, Peterborough in 2011 after a huge fire two years earlier but the theatre closed just five months later.
Coxwell, 29, of High Wycombe, admitted fraud at Peterborough Crown Court.
Despite being disqualified from being a director due to a previous fraud conviction, he had changed his name and went on to set up three companies with the aim of reopening the theatre.
BBC Look East's Louise Hubball was in court.

***

The press was saying that I left the show purely to do Dancing on Ice, but this was not the case. I just couldn't afford to carry on. Tell me anyone who will work for free, or worse still have to pay out of their own pocket to go to work.

Anyway, I walked away from that whole bad episode and began to experience the magic that was 'Dancing on Ice'. I had been approached to do it the year before, but I wasn't lucky enough to make it through. I think it was because they had Gareth Gates that year; he had danced with Maria who was to be my dance partner for this series. I guess Gareth and myself were too similar – both cut from the same cloth - and Gareth was seen as the better bet that year. That's show business.

Once I started rehearsing I knew it was going to be difficult, but I didn't want to lose. I was in it to win it, and from the minute I put my skates on I was focused. I didn't know yet who else was in the show and I was getting desperate to know who my competitors were.

For the first day of proper rehearsals I was with my manager and I was sweating with nerves. I was using muscles I didn't even know I had, but I wanted to impress the directors and the people that ran the show. So off I went, skating around the ice as fast as I could to make an impression, but as it turned out it had the opposition effect. They wanted me to slow down and be more in control: I was just like a mad cannon ball!

I was born in1988 when Torvill and Dean won the Olympics and I'd watched the show on TV in previous years, so I knew very well who they were. I was practising with Charlotte, a lovely girl and gorgeous looking. We went to Queensway Ice Rink, and she started to help me skate on my own. I remember putting my skates on the first time and they killed me to bits - I had blisters on blisters!

We were given the option of skating in a sectioned-off area, or being amongst the general public who were using the rink. There weren't many people there that day so we decided to skate on the main rink. One young couple couldn't skate at all: they were like a couple of Bambi's with legs and arms everywhere. Suddenly the lad fell over and his partner skated over his hand and took his index finger right off! I was like, 'Oh my God!' and it suddenly hit home how dangerous this was going to be for me if I wasn't careful. I skated straight over to them and the poor lad was in shock, just lying there holding his hand. I helped him up and Charlotte picked up the end of his finger. There was blood all over the ice and they had to rush him to hospital to fix him: it was a nightmare. Oh God! I thought again. What have I let myself in for!

Later on, once we'd started our first lesson, my teacher came up to me and said, "I'm not being funny Ray, but you skated over there in a panic and picked that lad up without any skating training whatsoever. You're going to be fine."

I suppose I'm naturally quite fearless, and I knew the only way this was going to work was to be up for the challenge. Compared with dancing, though, skating was a whole different ball game. For one thing I had to retrain myself to spin on the spot. There are a lot of things that people don't know about ice skating, one of them being that you spin on the spot but you kept your head straight. In dancing though, you do a thing called 'spotting' where you bring your head round before your body. So I had to retrain, and move away from all the stuff that I knew and had been being doing for years.

I'm quite good at disciplining my body and it started to become easier. Only a few weeks after getting on the ice the first time for real and just doing circuits around the rink, I was introduced to my real dancing partner. I was given no say as to who she would be, and we had six to eight weeks to prepare for Week One, but they couldn't have chosen anyone better. Chris and Jayne have been doing it for years, and they certainly know who to put with whom. Maria Filippov is Bulgarian and she was amazing. As a person she is proper sound - my type of girl! We had a real laugh and we just got on. I started to really enjoy myself, and not only was it fun, but it got easier and easier.

With Maria though, there were certain lifts she wouldn't do because of her past experience with Gareth Gates. In the last series he had got a lift wrong and seriously injured her knee. I was used to trusting my dance partners and having them trust me, so it never entered my head that Maria wouldn't feel the same. I think if the bond of trust is not there, this can open you up for accidents. If you are not 100% committed, then you are not committed at all, even though some of the moves can be a bit tricky and can hurt like hell if you get them wrong.

I wasn't an ice skater so my ability was in question, and I didn't like that. Knowing that I was capable of doing what they asked of me, I wanted Maria to trust me completely. That's my nature, and I was so determined to be the best. Of course, as the weeks went by there would be times when you were doing your best and nothing seemed to be improving, but then it clicked. After practice and more practice, the practice made perfect. It's my belief that putting in the effort always pays off.

As soon as I started the competition, saw the other contestants and could judge my own ability against them I could see that actually I skated pretty well. I even felt confident that if I kept my head down I could probably win easily. Maria had been on the programme before: she had started in the Australian version and won, and she'd also done the year before with Gareth Gates but bashed her knee proper when he dropped her. He wasn't a dancer and wasn't trained to do the things asked of him; it's dangerous to put someone on the ice without any training and make them responsible for another person's safety. Not only that, but within 8 to 10 weeks they are expected to perform to a standard it takes years to perfect. I guess I did have an advantage there. I've been told that each week I looked like I'd nailed it, but I knew I wasn't perfect every week, though I certainly tried my hardest. We were set a Challenge for each show, and if we carried it off we got extra points. I was working hard for those.

Being in a show like Dancing on Ice is a funny thing because you become part of a 'show biz bubble'. The outside world is a scary place, and you're just happy to be within the walls of your surroundings; for months you go to the ice rink, or studio, and you are around the same people on a daily basis until it become like a little home and family. It's very intense though, as there are a lot of huge characters - people not getting on, people getting on and people falling out. A lot went on for sure, but I kept quiet.

It was reported in the press 'Dancing on Ice Stars Give Ray Quinn the Cold Shoulder Because He's So Smug.' They were reporting that I was being accused of being fake, that I had an unfair advantage because of my dancing background and that I did not socialise with the rest of the cast. Yes, I was focused to win. Yes, I did practice a lot. Yes, I didn't socialise with the cast, as at the time I did not go out and I didn't really drink. I had Emma at home and we were madly in love with each other. Maybe now I wouldn't be so intense but again, I was young and I knew no different. I had been on the dancing scene since an early age and this is the most competitive game to be in. If I could turn back the clock I would still go all out to win the competition, but maybe I would have a bit of fun with the rest of the contestants at the same time.

We all stayed in same hotel, but I was living in London so only used my hotel room the night before and the night after the show. I was losing a lot of weight with all the cardio fitness every day, and it was fantastic. I may have lost a bit too much - my mum would say I was wasting away! -but I have never ever felt that fit in my life, I was totally ripped, I loved it.

Philip Schofield and Holly Willoughby from the Good Morning show were the presenters. It was weird really, cos we only saw them when we were actually at work, so to speak. You got to say hello, but I didn't get to know them or their families or anything. They didn't tend to hang around with the contestants, who all got stuck in and socialised. That first year I was so focused on what I was doing that I turned into a bit of a recluse. I really wanted to win, and my wife wanted to keep me out 'the bubble', so I wasn't influenced by anyone else. The other contestants were happy to party on tour but I never really went out drinking - just to the gym or the ice rink. I suppose I was boring really, but I just wanted to be the best I could every night, and to win.

When we went on tour with Dancing on Ice there was a winner every night, and a trophy was awarded, and I wanted to win as many as I could, the maximum you could achieve was 33. One year Chris Fountain achieved winning 26 out of 33 - and I wanted to beat that - I won 31 out of 33. I was happy.

I ended up winning the TV show and felt great, it was so cool that within my career I had been recognised for something that I was doing, my album had been out but had now dipped at bit in the charts, though I saw no revenue from the sales, all the money went to 'Syco' and Simon Cowell. Some of the tracks from the Album have been used in TV and Cinema and I see nothing of it. That was the contract I signed and I cannot begrudge it, no one forced me to sign.

I remember Emma finding some of my Albums in a bargain bucket at a petrol station on the motorway once. When she told me about it, we bought them all up as I was a bit embarrassed that that was where my album had ended up. I still had a lot of growing up to do.

Now that I had won Dancing on Ice I felt like I was back, back in the public eye - I had got my profile back maybe not in music but it was great, I was on the right route, I was back out there and people were talking about me. It was funny at the time that the media photo shots of me were wearing a t shirt that had been ripped, and underneath I was proper ripped. The picture got a bit publicity but I still looked young, maybe I was paranoid, but that I thought maybe people were thinking that's little Ray Quinn but his now got a bit of a body on him! It felt strange really. I had this proper fit, ripped body with a teenagers head on it. I still looked very young for my age.

My Manager Peter Brooks from my agency CAM got me that job I had been with them for years, and I haven't got a bad word to say about them and Peter himself was brilliant, But I got to a point in my career where I needed to move on, I left on good terms and I think he was a little disappointed as was I, I guess, that I felt the need to leave, as we had just had one of the best financial years to date. But life moves forward, I felt ready but and it was a hard decision to make.

Emma and I took holidays to the Maldives I bought new cars, I was buying Rolex watches and diamond ear rings - you name it, we were buying it. I spent a lot of money. I like to treat people and I like to treat people to watches as I am into watches myself. I bought my brothers matching watches, one had a white face the other was black. They were both worth about £500 each and both of them opened them, then looked at me and said thanks. Our Darren turned to me and said. "It's not that we don't appreciate it mate, but watches.

We would have appreciated a few more beers and a day at the race track with one of your flash motors."

I look back at it now, and they were right, what did they want with a couple of watches, a day racing around a track in a car followed by a few beers would have been a lot more fun and appreciated by them.

I also remember buying my dad a Citizen watch, it was not cheap. He opened the box and looked at the watch and then said. "Thank you son." Then after a pause went. "Citizen? What's that, is that good? To be honest son, not the watch I would have chosen for myself, but thanks it nice, thanks." With that he put it down, he now wears it all the time. It does make me smile thinking back. My dad is just my dad and there is no changing him and I would not want to.

My mum had a £1 nurses watch she had bought on the market, I will not go into what her view is of my watch fascination.

***

At the end of 'Dancing On Ice' we had a couple of weeks break and then we went on tour with the show, my manger phoned to tell me that the production company of Grease wanted me to return to the show. In my mind I was not too impressed I didn't want to go backwards, I needed to keep myself out there and keep moving forward.

My manager Peter called "We need to have a chat about Grease." he said.

"To be honest Peter, I don't want to go back to Grease." I tried to explain.

"Ray they are offering you DANNY!"

I couldn't believe it; the lead role, a lead role I had dreamed of as a kid. I had to do it – it was a dream come true. I really wanted to do it.

I asked how much they were offering, when he told me, there was no need to discuss any further. I was 'Danny'.

When I went into the show I wanted Emma to come back as Sandy.

"Can you audition her as a normal," I asked the producers. "She doesn't want to be given the part on my say so, she wants to win it on her own accord." Emma is quite independent. She auditioned and got the role. As if she wouldn't, who were we trying to kid. She had the role on my say so. It was a dream for the two of us. That show lasted six months, Emma was contracted for twelve months and I extended for one and half months at the end. We were flying high.

Public reaction was amazing we were selling out every day. The theatre was packed with dancing, happy audiences, there was always a massive queue at the stage door waiting to see me it was just brilliant it was just the Boss.

We up graded our flat in Clapham to a five bedroom detached home in St Albans on 1.5 acre plot of land, it was beautiful and it was a brand new house with a gravel drive and everything you could dream of, I felt like I was on top of the world, I was 21. For my 21st birthday I had a big family party, I'm talking the whole shebang, we had anything we wanted. Not a penny was spared. It wasn't a celebrity do, it was just me being flash I guess. The party cost me around £21K, hey I was 21. I had a 007 cake and the whole atmosphere was decadent. I was on top of the world again. You would have thought from the Syco experience I would have learnt to be a bit more careful. Well yeah, life was good and again I thought this was not going to end.

I remember going to the Maldives where we had a suite with private pool, and a butler, it was outrageous the money I was spending, but I was young and living the dream. Emma was lapping it up with me. We were like teenagers in a sweetshop.

I'm back on top I thought I had a Boss car a Range Rover Sport, with the body kit all over it. It looked the nuts and I was so proud of it.

Chapter 11

Reality Bites

After Grease Peter Brooks my manager got me into pantomime again. This time I told them to make sure it was all legit and we were not going to have a repeat of Peterborough. The show I chose was with Joe Pasquale.

I went straight to rehearsals in Birmingham for 'Cinderella' with the very funny Joe Pasquale, he was sensational, Joe had just won 'I'm a Celebrity Get Me Out of Here', he was in the limelight at the time, the producer's must of spent a lot to get us both in this production. I Played Prince Charming. It was brilliant!

Joe Pasquale is still my mate today and if I ever want advice or help he will always help me. The first time I met him I knocked on his dressing room door, and I pushed it open slightly and called out "Hello"

"Is that you Ray?" He called out.

"Yep!"

"Come in, Love."

I walked straight in and there he was, sat there on the couch with his baggy boxers on and his big old saggy bollocks hanging out. "Welcome to pantomime, Son!" he said, at which he burst out laughing, knowing that he had shocked me. I was crying my eyes out laughing.

"So you're Joe - you're a fucking nutter, Mate!"

"Ah, that's just who I am!' He smiled. 'We fuck about and we get paid. It's fucking great." Then continued to laugh at his own statement.

The first day in rehearsals I was totally star-struck by Joe because obviously I had grown up with him being on TV; he was a big name, and he'd just got out of the jungle as well. So many people warm to Joe, as he is who he is, and very honest with it. He is one of the nicest guys I have met in showbiz. I didn't have tattoos back then, but Joe had loads and I guess it became an instant talking point for us. In time we got closer and more relaxed; I opened up to him regarding my career, and he had been there, done it all. I wanted advice, and actually it was my dad who suggested Joe, with his long and varied career, would be a good person to get it from.

What Joe told me was, always listen to yourself. Don't take any directions from others, just follow your heart. Ignore all the bullshit in this industry - know who your friends are and trust no-one. Always remember to take care of your mum and dad and know they love you, no matter what. We had a lot of laughs during that time in the pantomime. I was still a bit of a baby, so my part in the show may have been a bit stage school. I was still only 21 and I've learned a lot since then. The other thing I learnt from Joe was about how to deal with fans. Some fans can be demanding; they think they know you and come in for a hug before they've even introduced themselves. They can be rather personal at times and to be truthful, as I am not really a social creature, it would often catch me unawares. The shows I had been in so far had kept the fans at arm's length. Joe helped me become more relaxed about it, knowing how to handle them and get out of situations I wasn't comfortable in. I remember one time he was being followed by a fan with a camera and he ended up getting his own camera-phone out and following them back. As I said, he is a funny guy!

There are some fans out there that really get involved with what you do. They buy all the merchandise, wear the T-shirts, turn up to gig after gig. I find it very flattering and try and do my best to please them, unlike some people in the business who take advantage of their 'celebrity' status. I was never a party animal in those days.

With the internet now, Facebook, Twitter and other social media, the fans can get even closer to you, or that is the perception for them. I am flattered that people have created web sites for me and about me that help inform everyone what I am doing. I try my best to keep them up to speed as to what I'm up to every minute of the day. A lot of my fans have stayed very loyal and I would not have the life I have today if it was not for all them standing by me, for which I am so very grateful for.

After the pantomime came to a close though, I was again out of work with no firm offers on the table. The rent on the house was £2.2K a month, and with no money coming in we had to let it go.

Post panto we moved back to Liverpool for 3 months with all our stuff, so we had a base for Emma, as her contract on Grease had also come to an end. We moved into the house in Liverpool that I had bought with my Brookside money – at the time we thought it would be the best thing to do.

Then an audition came up for 'Dirty Dancing' in the West End. It was a hard slog, as I had to do five auditions in total before I got the part of 'Billy Kostecki' - not the best role in the show. I wanted to be one of the dancers, but because I was known for what I was known for which was singing, I had to be the singer. It was a bit of drag singing the same songs every night for 8 months.

Emma quickly got frustrated in Liverpool, not wanting to be stuck there while I was in London, so we moved into a small flat in London which Emma's friends had been renting off a friend of theirs. They had bought another flat in the same building, and we got the opportunity to take it on at mate's rates. It was a one bedroom flat though, which was a big change from the five bedroom house we had been in not more than four months ago.

At the start of Dirty Dancing I was well into it but after three weeks it became routine, and just like a job. It was quite a depressing time in my life as I felt no enthusiasm for what I was doing. I wasn't motivated. I wasn't driven, and I had no creative control. The show I was in, involved doing the same thing every night to the same sort of audience every night. I was drinking too much, and I felt I was not where I should be in my career. I should have been enjoying what I loved to do. I was only happy when I was at home with Emma, hiding away, though she would moan at me for drinking too much. I was putting on the pounds, I couldn't be motivated to go to the gym. I was only happy when I was buying things for myself or others. I look back at this time now and know that I was searching for contentment. In essence, I was pretty depressed with everything that was around me. I ended up doing a 12 month stint with Dirty Dancing as an extension of my original contract of six months.

After that I ended up going back into pantomime again in 'Jack and the Beanstalk' at the Royal & Derngate in Northampton with Emma as my co-star. My fee was half of what it had been the year before, and I was starting to get really down. Was this my life? - West End show then Pantomime? Don't get me wrong: I enjoyed the pantomimes, the fun on stage and the crowd participation, the young kids faces beaming with joy, but I felt there was more to me than this.

It was at this time that I got engaged to Emma. I was in love, and she was the only one for me. I bought the ring in London, from Tiffany's just off Bond Street, and I took it back with me to the pantomime in Northampton. It wasn't until we went down to Poole where her parents lived that I popped the question. On Christmas Day I made up a story to take her out in the car, and I took her to a bench overlooking Sandbanks that her grandfather used to sit on. This was where I asked her to marry me: she was so happy she cried her eyes out - I was happy too, I can tell you!

We moved out of the one Bedroom flat into a basement flat in Blackheath. It was slightly bigger but still not perfect.

Georgie phoned me up and told me that they wanted

me back in 'Dirty Dancing'. There were no other offers on the table, so I thought I may as well go back to that, as at least it was a paying job.

Emma was starring in 'Dreamboats and Petticoats' at the time, so we had money coming in.

I hated getting the London Underground, not because it is public transport, I just hate the tube. I hate the crowds, the unreliability of it. So I decided to buy myself a motorbike, it was a Triumph Street Triple R, it was a great bike and it was fast and perfect to get about in town. Then I had my accident.

I went out one Sunday for a casual ride; it was a sunny day with a bit of a drizzle and I left Emma at home, as I just wanted to get some air.

I remember it being a busy Sunday - maybe there football match on or something. A woman pulled out in front of me, as I went to put on the breaks my front wheel locked and I went skidding off and broke my collar bone; it snapped in two halves. I hadn't had the bike long, and I wasn't used to it. When the ambulance came I was put on a stretcher and taken off to A&E where they strapped me up and said, "Go home and give it four weeks, and you should start to get better."

It didn't get better though, so asked if I could have an operation to fix it. I was losing money all the time and I needed to get back to work. I'd already been off for more than 6 weeks, and my sick pay went down to £38 a week for 12 weeks. Meanwhile I had rent to pay and no other source of income. It was a twelve week waiting list unless I went private, but obviously at my own cost. I had bike insurance but they advised that because it was a big case with loss of earnings involved it would take a while to come through. 'Oh God! I thought, how long?' I had a tax bill to pay at the end of the year, and a lot of outgoings. I couldn't wait another twelve weeks with no money, so I went private: £4k it cost and I was in the very next day, and then within 2-3 weeks I was back at work.

I couldn't finish my contract with 'Dirty Dancing', as it had expired by then, so I started rehearsing in Darlington North Yorkshire for another pantomime. I didn't take out personal insurance for that, even though my management did ask me once. Like any other young man, I thought I was indestructible and everything would always be alright: it was expensive too and I didn't think I needed it.

I was then contacted by Georgie and asked if I would do 2 weeks in Grease in the Liverpool Empire and it was during these two weeks that 'Harry' was conceived. It must have been something to do with the Liverpool air.

I then started doing pantomime in Darlington where I played Prince Charming in Cinderella, and once again Emma was my co-star, but had to pull out for the last week because this was when we found out she was six weeks pregnant. I remember buying four or five pregnancy test kits to double check that Emma really *was* pregnant! We weren't planning for it, but we weren't being careful to prevent it either, so when we found out I was excited, but nervous. This was going to change my life, and I was going to have to grow up pretty quick.

After the pantomime was over I went on tour with 'Legally Blonde', but I was starting to get less and less for each show I appeared in. There was nothing I could do about it, though. The thing with show biz is that you have to stay current, and I was not. I remember phoning up CAM Management and saying, "What's going? Is this all I'm going to be doing? Isn't there anything else out there?" Legally Blonde was another show that I got depressed on, and I started putting on weight. Emma was at home and I just want to be with her as much as possible and would try to get home as much as I could.

I played Warner Huntington III, and fair enough it was a great show. It was an OK tour, though not a sell-out, and in many ways I enjoyed it.

Les Denis was in it with me, and we got on really well and had some fun. We used to chip in together and get to stay in decent places during the tour.

It was during the Legally Blonde tour that I got married to Emma. We flew out to Barbados and the wedding took place on a tiny little beach at the back of our hotel. Emma's mum and dad and her three sisters and little brother were there, and my mum came out but my dad wasn't well enough. I spent the night before the wedding with mum in a hotel. She asked me. "Is this what you want, Son? I can't believe my little boy is getting all grown up."

"I told her I was over the moon, and yes - this was defiantly what I wanted!" In reality though I was scared, I didn't know what I wanted, I think I knew I wanted to marry Emma though. There were reports in the press that I didn't have the body language of a young man marrying the love of his life, but that is the press for you. It was hot, I was nervous and I was getting married!

We spent about two weeks in Barbados on our honeymoon. Of course, Emma was now six months pregnant and on our wedding night we went to bed at 9 because by then she was done in. It was a nice relaxing time and it was great to spend time with Emma on our own enjoying food and the surroundings. At the time I was enjoying my food *too* much though, and looking back at my wedding photos I can see that I was bloated and out of shape, but I was content with Emma and I had a baby on the way.

When we got back I went out on tour again with 'Legally Blonde', finishing in July that same year. At this stage of my career I was feeling a little lack–lustre; there was no excitement to what I was doing. I wanted to try something else: I wanted to get into acting, and I wanted to be taken seriously and play a serious role. My agent at the time said, 'Think of Sheridan Smith – she'd only done one play in the West End with Keira Knightley and after that she went from strength to strength,' so they sent me to do an audition for 'Rise and Fall of Little Voice.' I got the part of Billy and I had to take a low rate, but at the time I wanted to get into acting and focus on one thing. I was doing so many other things that were not working, so I went into acting in the belief that this offered greater longevity for my career. At this time I was also quickly running out of money.

In the show with me were Beverley Callard and Jess Robinson. The director was supposed to be Jim Cartwright, which was why I took the job, as he was head honcho in the acting world. He was one of the best writers in the UK, but the producers had a bit of a fall out with Jim and I heard on the grapevine that it was to do with money. Anyway, Jim pulled out of the project and his young assistant took over as director. After that the show was fraught with incidents. For one thing, Paul McGann was sacked early on for being too rough on-stage with Beverley; he said it was method acting, but Beverley wasn't happy. He had a number of warnings and then he was let go, with the press reporting that he had left the show for other commitments.

Beverley Callard was still not happy and called the cast into a meeting. 'I just want to talk about Jim,' she said. 'Certain things in our contract have not been fulfilled and Jim Cartwright is one of them. I feel that Jim has been hard done by. After all, he wrote the play, not the production. If you're all up for it, I think we should stand together and refuse to go on stage unless Jim is heavily involved.'

After the meeting, the replacement for Paul McGann wasn't happy with what Beverley had suggested and said he was going to stick with the show, as this was a big opportunity for him. When he stuck with it so did the rest of the cast; I just went along with them, as I didn't want to rock the boat, and in the end Beverley stayed too.

As the show was coming to its end the producer decided he wanted to extend it by six months. We were told that he might re-cast, but meanwhile he asked us to let him know whether or not we would be happy to stay. As I was skint at the time and had nothing else on the table, I had no option but to carry on. It was at this time that I had to drop my manager, Georgie. I couldn't afford to pay 30% of my wages over to them if I was going to do the extension for the same money. I did ask for more, but the producers wouldn't wear it, and I already owed Georgie from previous contracts. Having a manager was all I'd ever known, so I was now about to venture into uncharted waters. I had a meeting with Georgie to explain that I couldn't afford to keep her and an agent. She was very understanding, but it took me a while to settle my account with them, as I had run up quite a bill for monies that I owed them on commission - £20K in fact.

At the same time I had emails coming through on my phone telling me that I owed money for this and money for that. I thought, I have a child on the way, I responsibilities to pay for and I owe money, so I paid my bills as a priority; I paid my tax, I paid my accountant. I really had no money left now, and I definitely had no money in my account to pay Georgie, so I decided to ask her if they were ok with me to pay them if and when I could.

I remember sitting in the car with Emma and willing myself to be strong enough to get on the phone. Georgie answered the phone right away, and I explained that I had paid all the bills I could and with a baby on the way and a family to support I was now seriously short of cash. Would she and her partner be happy for me to pay them if and when I could? Georgie said that was perfectly ok - that she and Richard adored me and they did not want me worrying about this bill. I was so relieved, but now I had to tell them that my next role wasn't paying enough money, and I would have to leave the management team altogether. "If you're going to leave us," she said, "that's fine. But let me warn you that there's no easy way back in."

This was all happening around the time our Harry came along – a healthy 7llb 7 ½ ounce baby. He was born in Poole Hospital, on the 2nd August, 2012 at 7:45 in the morning, after 21 hours labour. I was there for the delivery and cut the cord and everything, and I felt very proud of Emma and a bit in shock that I was now the 22 year old father of a baby boy. I remember holding him in my arms and thinking, 'I'm one of the youngest people on this ward!' Then a heavily pregnant girl of about 13 carrying a pink Game Boy walked in with her mother, and this made me feel better – at least I was not the youngest there!

Sadly my nan did not live long enough to see Harry born, which was devastating for me; I'd been so close to her and she had always been there to support me through thick and thin. My first tattoo was a guardian angel, which I had done in honour of Nan by Kevin Paul, a guy in Derby who was recommended to me by my agency at the time. All my tattoos are done by Kevin now. I did have one done in Jersey of a compass pointing North East, but Kevin has since redone it.

I now had a young mouth to feed and I was lucky that my management had agreed to let me pay the money when I had it. To be honest, I wasn't good with money at the best of times. When I was paid I should have taken what I owed the management and put it in a reserve account, but I just spent everything as it came into the bank. Since then I have met people that have very good accountants and a close relationship with them; they don't do anything with their money unless the accountant agrees to it. My accountant at the time was not only expensive, but told me he was not a financial adviser. I just went with it, but looking back I should have questioned what was going on, looked into my spending - I should have had a financial strategy in place. It was money coming in and I spent it, but in my view the accountant messed up my affairs big time. I remember getting a big tax bill one year that I didn't know was coming, and this totally wiped out my bank account. I was skint!

If I had done this on day one, or someone had sat me down and made me do it I would be in a lot better place financially now than I am. It isn't that I wasted the money on a wild life style I just didn't use it to the best of its ability. If I went back in time now, did Emma and I really need a five bed room house for the two of us? Really?

My accountant was expensive at the time and had told me he was not a financial adviser. I just went with it as I just stuck to the people that were given to me at the start of my career. Looking back now I should have questioned what was going on, looked into my spending. I should have had a financial strategy in place. The only person to blame in reality is myself. I could have asked anyone, I could have read up on it, I could have got independent advice. All I needed to do was pick up the phone, but my head was deeply buried in the sand. I didn't know that you had to pay your taxes in arrears. This year had not been a good one for me income wise, but the year before had been a bumper one: this was the year I owed the tax for.

I carried on with the 'Rise and Fall of Little Voice.' To my surprise Beverley stayed with the show too, even after what she had said at the beginning. As for me, to be honest I had to stay because I needed the money and there was nothing else out there for me. I now had a child and a wife to support, and I went on tour with Emma and a 5 week old baby in tow. We weren't staying in the best places - all one bedroom flats in basements, or buildings with a make-shift flat. I remember one time having to put all the electric heaters in one room to keep Harry warm. Of course, Emma couldn't go anywhere because Harry was just a babe in arms; at this stage he hadn't even learned to crawl. It was hard for all of us. I had to do two shows a day and Emma was in places she did not know.

Over Christmas I did Aladdin in Poole. This was a welcome break for Emma as she could spend some time with her parents, and they helped with looking after Harry. I was the only known star in that pantomime, but again my fees were halved from the year before. It was the usual run of the mill show, but they are always fun to do, and it's great to watch the kids' reactions in the audience -the smiles, the laughs and all the screaming! I always remember my time watching Peter Pan with my mum and in every audience there were kids like I was then, aspiring to be on the stage. Many of the kids would one day enter drama school and start on this life style.

During the tour of 'Rise and Fall of Little Voice' we were in our flat in Poole and I made a decision that had been brewing for a while, which was to get rid of CAM and Peter Brooks. It was like having a break up having to phone them and tell them I didn't want to be with them any more. Peter was very shocked. "I can't quite believe where all this is coming from! I thought we were doing really well - I got you the tour." But for a long time I'd felt like I wasn't going anywhere with them; I had some space now, and I was going to try something different. Stuart Piper was managing Jess Robinson who was in the show with me. I contacted him on Facebook, and knowing Jess and knowing I was looking for new management Stuart jumped at the chance. He asked Jess to give me his number so that I could give him a call, and when I did we had a good chat. "I heard you were looking for new representation," he said. "I've seen you on the TV, and I admire you and I think you have a talent. I believe we are the right team for you to get you where you want to be."

I said I'd been looking at his client list, and seen that a lot of them were current. "I want to be that guy on the TV!" I said. Of course, I was saying all the wrong things! I was trying to be the type that goes on 'I'm a Celebrity' and all that, but in reality this was *not* where I wanted to be. I was just getting desperate.

"Absolutely, Ray! I see you doing all those things, and I see you presenting. You're a lovable guy - you do have that likeability factor." He said encouragingly.

"Can you tell me then, if I was to go with you, are there things going that I could be put up for?"

"Absolutely Ray! There are things out there that I could put you in for right now." He sounded like a cheap, car salesman.

"Fantastic!" I said. "I feel quite good now. I was a bit

apprehensive about leaving me last agent, because they were so good for me. But after what you've told me, I think I'm making the right decision. Let me talk it over and sleep on it and I'll be back in touch."

Sure enough, I phoned Stuart the following day saying, "I think you are the ones for me and I'm pleased to be joining a younger, trendier agency that's more in the spot light. I've had a chat with Emma of course, and I was thinking that maybe you could speak to her about coming on board too."

"Yeah, that's great news! Tell Emma to come in and have a chat when she's ready. In the meantime, great to have you on board! I'll get one of the girls in the office to send over all the paperwork."

Emma was pleased when I said Stuart wanted to meet her. She came up with the idea that we should pitch something to them as a couple thing. Maybe we could do some presenting together. I agreed with Emma at the time and we had some photos done and sent them across to Stuart. Nothing ever came of it, though.

The 'Little Voice' tour finished in June 2013. By then the show had got me down; I'd put on more weight and I was just not in a place I wanted to be. During the tour I'd been offered Peter Pan at the Liverpool Empire that Christmas. I asked them to consider Emma for the lead girl, and she got the job. They paid us a good wage and Emma was back in work.

Between the end of Little Voice and Peter Pan I did some minor gigs with Butlins and Pontins. These were for X Factor nights and being introduced as Ray Quinn from the X Factor, and paid me a good bit of money towards clearing my debts. In October, 2013 while driving around the country doing these gigs for Butlins and Pontins I was travelling back home one night and this track came on the radio: 'I Giorni' by Ludovico Einaudi. It really upset me at the time, and I starting talking to my nan in my head. I was asking for her for some guidance and telling her that if only I could get something like 'Dancing on Ice' again I would be able to get back on top. The very next day I got a phone call from Stuart Piper. "I don't know how much of it is true," he said, "but there's a rumour that they're bringing back Dancing on Ice and they are doing a Champions of Champions. All the winners from the series will be competing against each other."

I couldn't believe it. "Shut up - you're joking!"

"Well, I don't know if it's true, and I don't know yet if it's happening."

As soon as I put the phone down, I called Jayne Torvill and asked her if it was true that there was a version of 'Dancing in Ice' coming back on. She told me it was true, and asked me if I was in. I told her of course: I would be there and I would win it! I would be the best! Then she asked me if I was with an agent. I told her I was, but if they were doing this and it was the same as before, I would really rather do it myself. She told me she loved me and it would be great to have me on the show. If I wanted to do it on my own, she would get the producers to contact me direct. I told her I'd better not though, as I didn't want to piss Stuart off. A week later Stuart called to tell me 'Dancing on Ice' was happening; it was going to be called 'Dancing on Ice All Stars' and the producers wanted to meet me on Thursday to discuss the show.

"We are here because we have new and exciting news. We are going into the last series of Dancing on Ice and we want to finish with a bit of a bang. We are bringing all the 'winners' and past 'runner ups' chosen by Chris and Jayne for the final All-Stars series of 'Dancing on Ice.'"

I sat there with a straight face, waiting for her next words. She looked at me as if she had just told me the best new in the world and was now surprise I didn't react in the excited way she was obviously expecting.

"What? Is there something wrong?" She asked.

"No I told her. This is the best news I have heard, but I had known about it a few weeks ago, as I had already spoken to Jayne."

"Oh thank god! I thought you was going to tell me that you wasn't interested." She told me with some relief.

We then started discussing the show and I told her how much I wanted to do it. In the back of my brain I was thanking my nan for looking out for me. I really needed this to happen. It was when they told me they were 90 percentage confident it was going to happen, I started to have a niggling panic but I didn't show it. This is one of those times in life where you are touching the light at the end of the tunnel and it could so easily have been switched off by one of the money men in ITV.

I had an anxious wait for a few weeks until the show was confirmed that it was actually going on air.

I was used to have a team around me, but now I was on my own. I would turn up in my car, walk through the slot machines to do these gigs. At these sort of places they did not have a stage door. You turned up and just spoke to the DJ or Manager and he would show you back stage.

It was Andy Pountain who had set these gigs up for me. He had been with me during the X-Factor days. They were a far cry from those days but they were my bread and butter and they were saving my life at the time, and for that I was very grateful.

When the pantomime 'Peter Pan' started I moved Emma, Harry and her mother up to Liverpool. We rented two flats next to each other. One for Emma and I and one for her mother. We got them on short leases. Emma and I did the show together, we never went out, and would always be in with Harry, and her mother. We got a fee as a couple which was handy for us.

During the pantomime I was training for Dancing on Ice, I was in the rink every morning at 6am and finished at 9am practicing with Maria. It was good to be back skating with her and good for my waist line and fitness! I was now buzzing again and looking after myself. Emma and Harry came to the ice rink once for filming but didn't come any other times.

After practicing on the ice I would go to pantomime rehearsals which was followed by the live shows. Really tough days but it was good to be working this hard.

I had to miss the last two days of pantomime due to the 'Dancing on Ice' schedule so I lost that money, but it was good to be back on the show.

The show brought back most of the 'winners' and 'runner ups' from the past series. It was great to be with such talent. I was also with some good old friends such as Joe Pasquale who sadly went in round two. Gareth Gates was also on the show and I got on really well with him. It was not all about the skating as Todd Carty was in the show!

I smashed it again, I was on the top the leader board for most of the shows. I ended up in the bottom two the week before the final, but got through on judges votes.

I won the final, so this was the second time I'd won Dancing on Ice. I had been focused throughout the show and again, didn't socialise and would go back home for the week. On the Friday and Saturday night I would stay in the Hotel in order that I was focused and rested and so Harry couldn't keep me up all night. Following the 'after show party', we went to the studio bar at Pinewood, everyone was there, my mum, our Sue, my dad was propping up the bar as usual. It was another really good night. Stuart, was there, he wanted free tickets to the final, but I told him that I only wanted my family there. He didn't watch the show but came to the bar afterwards with Shaun who was my PR guy. I was never really happy with my PR guy, he didn't get me much, he kept telling me that no-one was interested in me. He never said much else, never gave me any advice on how to get people interested in me, just kept bluntly telling me, no-one was interested.

I did a ten minute interview on TV the next day and not a lot of press. I had no offers coming in. It was not what I was hoping for.

I remember turning to Stuart on the night of the finals. He was only there for an hour. When we chatted outside briefly I said. "Right! Now I've done my bit, done what was asked of me, I have won the show, now it's your turn."

He told me throughout the show. "You have to win Ray, no pressure, but you are going to have to win, because then it will be amazing."

He said to me. "Oh absolutely you have exceeded yourself Ray, you were fantastic, and don't you worry there is plenty of stuff in the bag for you, there is loads of different things we can have you doing. I will tell you all about it tomorrow. By the way I have got you a pantomime."

I remember watching him at that party as he scouted around the room looking for people to network with and to try and drum up business for himself.

I waited for him to call me, I went home, chilled, and had some family time with Emma and Harry.

I phoned Stuart a week later to ask him what he had for me. "Right yeah, we have had a couple of things in for you, first of all, panto, they have come through and offered Aladdin in the Liverpool Empire."

"Yeah great, how much they offering?" I asked.

When he told me I remember thinking 'Blimey, that's not a lot!'

"I have told them, I said you obviously don't want Ray then, I am negotiating for you."

"Last time I won Dancing on Ice I got a hell of a lot more than that, come on Stuart!"

"I know buddy, leave it with me and I will sort it out for you."

"So, what else have you got?"

"He said erm…. I have erm… I have had a couple of guys… I erm have a script for you…"

"Script, what for..?"

"A play on tour,,, it is a really good part… I think you should look at it Ray."

"What else have you got?"

"I have a possibility of Emmerdale Ray..."

"I don't want to do a play on tour, I don't really want to do Emmerdale. Come on Stuart get me on current TV. I want to be main stream."

"Leave it with me Ray... I will sort it out." With that he hung up.

I thought, 'What a bullshitter!' I wasn't happy and here I was paying 20% of my commission to these guys and I got them the Dancing on Ice gig. I felt let down and again, used.

He phoned me back the next day and said he had doubled the money for the pantomime but it was still nowhere near the amount I had been paid the last time, but I said I would take it.

It was at this time I met a guy called Steve Coxshall in a pub in Hampstead. This guy was going to change my life completely but I had no idea at the time what impact he was going to have.

After my two weeks off I started touring with Dancing on Ice. In mid-March we started rehearsals and began the tour on 28th March which finished mid-April. We did 37 shows around arenas in the UK and I won most of the arena dates.

This time though I went out with the cast and crew on the nights out. Gareth Gates would take me out, and he seemed to know everyone and we would always end up being given free drinks. Gareth knew how to enjoy himself and I would go out alongside him. We got on really well.

I remember one time in rehearsals when we went to the gym together Gareth wanted some cigarettes on the way so we pulled into this garage and I jumped out to get a packet of Marlborough Lights for him from the counter and the lady behind it asked me for I.D. I didn't know what to say. I didn't want to use the line 'Don't you know who I am?' so I said. "The cigarettes are for the guy driving the car outside." Pointing at Gareth in his White Range Rover who was waving at us both. The lady behind the counter looked at me and said. "I still need to see some I.D."

I sacked Stuart half way through the tour, I was sitting in my dressing room surrounded by all the lads, and I knew half of them were going onto something else and here was me, I had just won the show and I've been off air now for about 5 weeks. I had nothing to follow this and there was nothing in the pipeline. I hadn't heard from Stuart for about 3 to 4 weeks, so I phoned up the agency and I asked if Stuart was back from his holiday yet. They told be no, but he should be in next Wednesday. As soon as I put the phone down, I drafted the following email.

To Stuart and Dom

With me being on tour, Having spent some time on my own, I've had time to think things over.
And I feel it's time for me to part ways with the agency, there are a number of reasons for this. Which I'm happy to explain.

I feel let down, I was promised way too much smoke and mirrors. Also communication is a tiring subject for me to indulge. I also feel pro activity is for me is not at the front of your minds.

You've not come to see me on tour to support what I've

*just achieved, and the phone isn't ringing off the hook.
I am aware the business is tough at the moment, so this
is not a personal thing, but I want to use this period in
my career to try and use the profile I have, which I have
learnt from previous experiences doesn't last long, and
needs to be used to the best advantage!*

*I've been more than fair with my timings and allowed
for things to happen, but I'm afraid the time has come
to move on!*

*I know you will understand this. Obviously the jobs I've
received through you*

I.E Panto, Doi etc you will take your commission.

*Please don't hesitate to call me with any question or
queries you have on this.*

*I thank you for the time you have spent up to this point
and there are no hard feelings.*

Kind regards

Ray Quinn.

No one responded to my email. I got a phone call from
Jonathan Schalit.

"Hi Ray, I have heard about the email sent to Stuart,
saying you want to leave. Have you got time to have a
chat?"

I said "Yeah I have time to chat, I feel totally let down,
I haven't heard from Stuart at all, they tell me he is on
holiday."

"Let me be straight with you Ray."

"I have suspended Stuart from the office for a seven
week break to allow him to get his head together. He's
really not well."

"What do you mean he is not well? What is wrong with him?"

"Well he is going through a divorce, and his head is all over the place and the moment."

I said "Fair enough he's going through a rough patch, but when was anyone going to tell me about it! The guy is supposed to be looking after my life! I'm not being funny Jonathan but I feel so let down. I know he's going through a lot and I can appreciate him going through it, but when was I going to be told that the guy who was looking after me and my livelihood, is not capable of doing it. Was I just going to be left on the shelf?"

"I thought Dom was looking after you."

"Dom is all very well and nice but she ain't my agent, she ain't out there getting the work for me. It's not good enough, when was I supposed to find about Stuart! I have worked my fucking arse off and now I'm back to square one."

"Well Ray, your such a talented guy, and when we had that initial meeting with you and Emma at the beginning the team upstairs were so excited with your enthusiasm and your ideas, and I am sorry you feel let down. So look I don't want an answer right now, but I want to offer your ROAR Global. You can come upstairs with me and you can seen what we have done with our clients. You will go in the magazine."

Roar Global have a glossy mag that goes to their selected clients. It was a major thing to be featured in this magazine as a star.

"Why was this not put in place weeks ago, what are ROAR going to do for me now. If you think I'm that talented Jonathan, why was ROAR not engaged with me when I was winning Dancing on Ice. Why has it taken me to open my gob, for you then to put me in ROAR. Thank you for your offer and I will go away and think about."

By this time I had already met my future manager, I had a think about it, spoke to Emma about it, and she was all for me joining ROAR, it was a big deal in her eyes.

I was sick of waiting around, I had gone through this sort of thing so many times before. I turned down the offer, with much deliberation and thought. I was scared, I had just turned down ROAR and in London they are huge.

I had a gut feeling what this was going to be like, despite all the advice around me, I turned him down. I had joined up with my new manager and that was it. I wanted to prove them wrong.

Holiday on Ice contacted Andy Pountain, my old agent, and asked me how much I wanted. I told him and got it. I was accepting jobs for the money, not for what I wanted to do.

Andy Pountain had 50 or so Butlins gigs lined up for me, but my new manager told he was not happy with me doing them. I knew I needed the money.

At this time I became ill, my throat was gone and I needed to stay in bed, there was no way I was going to be able to perform. I rang Andy up and told him I couldn't do the gig tonight because I was ill.

Andy was short on the phone, and said "Why are you letting me down. They are going to be pissed off with me Ray."

"I can't help it Andy I'm ill." And with that Andy hung up.

I then phoned my new manager and told him how Andy had been with me and he said, "Fuck it. Cancel all the gigs!"

"But I need the money mate." I explained.

"I need you to do other stuff, Ray."

"But it's a lot of money and I need the money."

"We will find the money."

So I cancelled some of the gigs. Andy was pissed with me. He ranted on about me letting him down.

I told my new manager to email him, and tell him that I didn't want to do any of the gigs at all. I then received an email from Andy stating that he had heard from my manager and asked if he was having a laugh.

I told him that he was right, this isn't what I want to do. I was on a new path now. Andy explained that I used to thank him for these gigs, this used to be my bread and butter, it was all about the money, and that he is now losing and would have to give the gigs away. The then told me to send him an email with a sick note attached.

I didn't want to let him down, but I had to listen to my new manager now. I wanted more, I wanted something different and my new manager had a plan.

He has sent me a couple of emails since. But I have not taken him up on any of his offers.

My new management took over all the contracts and appearances.

Holiday on Ice was Brighton and it was for a week. We rehearsed the show back in November in Amsterdam in Holland as this was where the tour was at the time and it had an Ice Rink I could use. I was in the show with loads of foreigners. Russian, Americans, Eastern Europeans it was a great culture mix.

I finished Pantomime on 4th Jan in Liverpool then travelled down to Brighton, and on the 6th did a dress run for a show that evening. I hadn't rehearsed or done anything connected to the show since November. I had a part, a script and a show to host.

I enjoyed my time in Brighton and drank with a couple of American guys also in the show.

Chapter 12

Steve Coxshall

I first got to know Steve Coxshall on Monday 23rd of April, 2014. We met through Jason Gardiner, who had been one of the judges on Dancing on Ice. The meeting was to talk about doing some nights in the Rabbit Hole, which is a small live music venue in the basement of the Duke of Hamilton pub in Hampstead. Steve had owned the Duke of Hamilton, a typical old-fashioned London pub, for five years. Prior to him taking over, the building had been under threat from a developer planning to turn it into flats. The locals had got up a petition to block that happening and Steve had taken it over and turned it around. Then in 2011 it won Best Pub in London.

After Dancing on Ice Jason had told me he had a really important project he wanted me involved in. He never told me what it was for ages and I was getting really excited; he made it sound really major, and I thought it was going to be the next big thing in my career. He arranged for us to meet up at 'the Duke' at ten am. Initially I expected a hotel, but I ended up arriving outside a pub. I thought, this can't be right, and I went to drive on but then I spotted Jason sitting outside with another guy, so I parked up and went over to meet them. My first impression of this other bloke, with all his rings and jewellery, was of another Del Boy out of Only Fools and Horses. I was asked if I wanted a drink and I was thinking, what the fuck is all this about? I was in a pub, and here was Jason with this guy who looked like some gangster. I wasn't comfortable at all.

Anyway, I sat down with a coke and Jason started to explain, "What we're going to do is downstairs here in the pub – we've converted it into a live lounge theatre." Then he turned to the other guy and said, "This is Cocky, and this is his pub!"

"Ok," I said. "So you own this pub."

Cocky – but I call him Steve, as 'Cocky' doesn't sound right! - told me that yes, he owned the pub and a number of other businesses. After doing twenty years in the city he had decided to change direction and calm his life down, so he'd bought the Duke. Jason explained that he had met Cocky through the National Television Awards in 2007. Cocky was there with Kyran Bracken (rugby union player), who was a friend, and they'd come up with the idea of setting up the Rabbit Hole Group to turn the downstairs of the Duke of Hamilton into a leading London entertainment venue. (At one time they'd been in talks with Alan Carr, Emma Bunton, Kelly Hoppen and others, but none of that came to anything, as in due course there was a fall out between Jason and Cocky and they went their separate ways.)

We sat and discussed what I was doing, and they told me they'd like me to do some nights downstairs. The venue has a capacity of 50 – not what I was expecting after the big build-up from Jason. This was just the basement of a pub in Hampstead! Anyway, I gave Steve my number before I left and that same evening he got in touch.

"Hope you don't mind me calling you, but you mentioned your talks with Warners. I've been reviewing where you are at the moment, and I don't think you should take the deal. I think there are better options."

"What do you mean?" I asked.

"Look Ray, I'm a business man; there are other ways of doing things. You've got a brand. I think we can put a number of nights on and fund the album with that: do it that way. Come along tomorrow - there's a producer Jason and I would like you to meet."

"Yeah, ok. That sounds alright."

I thought about what Steve had said. I had money in the bank, but the Warner's deal was a bit like vanity publishing: I took all the risk and if the album didn't sell, *I* would be the one out of pocket.

The following day I met Steve at the pub and then we picked up Jason at Kings Cross and walked what felt like miles to Tile Yard, where we met Shaun Hargreaves and went into his gorgeous studio. He introduced us to the music he does and told us who he had been working with. I was so excited to be back in a studio! I felt like a little kid, and I seemed to be getting on really well with Steve. After this Steve and Jason took me to the Horseshoe in Hampstead and over lunch I got to know Steve a little better. Jason asked me about my present management and then put it to me that they would be interested in taking me on.

Well, I turned round to them and said to Steve, "Let me go and have a think about this - my brain is in overload - and, with the greatest respect," I added hesitantly, "You're not really a typical music manager are you?" With that Steve looked at me and said, "You're right. I'm a businessman, and this isn't about the music, it is about business." He seemed a bit short with me at the time.

That night, though, he phoned me to say he wanted to manage me. He told me that music was a business, and that he needed to run it as such. "Your current management aren't doing you justice," he said. "You've just won 'Dancing on Ice' for the second time and what have they got on the table for you? Nothing!" There was a pause, and then he asked, "What do you want to do, Ray?"

"Well," I told him, "I want financial security more than anything, and on top of that I want a successful career and people realising I'm good. I don't want to have to keep proving myself and earning my place, only to be dropped every time."

"Look, we can do this!" Steve said. "If I'm your manager I can get you back. But I want you 100% - anything less won't work. I need to know everything about you: your income, your outgoings your debt, everything, because then I will help structure it for you and turn you into a business. There's a lot you can learn from me, but you have to listen to me. This will be tough; it'll be like starting again, but if you want it Ray, you can have it, and I will teach you how to get it."

It was a lot to take in. He obviously liked my energy, liked who I was, and at the time my head was wrecked.

I was on a low and this guy was happy to dedicate his life to me and try and get me to where I wanted to be. He told me to watch the film Jerry McGuire, as in all essence this is what we were going to do.

I went away to think things over. I spoke to Steve again and he told me that he'd have a strategy put in place within two or three days. When I asked Emma what she thought her first question was, "What has he done?" I told her he had worked with 'Blue', that he knew the right people and that he was really passionate about me and what we could achieve together. Anyway, all the agencies, managers and the like that I had been with so far had kept me hanging, and I'd never really been happy that they were doing the best for me.

'What have I got to lose?' I thought, so I agreed to have Steve manage me. I dropped all my other management and now it was just Steve and I taking on the world - on our own, and as unit!

***

A couple of days later I received a text from Steve saying he had really exciting news for me and to come down the pub, as he wanted to tell me face to face. When I arrived there was the usual summer crowd in. We went down the road to have a burger, and on the way to the burger joint I said, "Come on, Steve! For fucks sake, what's the news?"

"You're going to love me!"

"Why, for fucks sake? What is it?"

"We're going to New York! And we're going to a studio to get some tracks recorded with a top producer.

Warners are looking for a project like you and we're going to send them some recordings."

"Shit, Man! How we going to pay for it?"

"Well, you're going to do six nights in the Rabbit Hole, and that'll fund the trip and the recording."

The tickets were £50, and we sold out every night. It was a really cool place to do a gig, plus Steve had me doing meet and greets. It was good to know that people would come and see me for a premium price; this was the first time in a while that I felt good again, and Steve had proven that he really could deliver what he said he could. Jason turned up to one of the shows with Gemma Sheppard, (x factor stylist) but it was after this evening that Jason and Steve fell out and Steve went on his own.

Apart from meeting the fans at the Duke of Hamilton, I also came into contact there with some of the people who would be entering my new life in a big way. It was at one of these gigs that I met my publishers, who had been invited along with their teenage author Lilly Say. They gave Emma a signed copy of Lilly's children's book for our Harry. Little did I know how much time I would be spending with them in the not very distant future.

***

New York, July 2014

When Steve and I arrived in New York we checked into our hotel, and as we were not in the studio until the following day I suggested we went out for some food and couple of beers. The night turned into a few more beers than I could normally drink though, and he drunkenly suggested we find a strip club. The cab driver took us to place called Flash Dance and two girls there, one from Manchester and the other from Brighton, recognised me from the X Factor. That was as far as it went: we had a quick chat and a few beers and made our way back to the hotel. We were not due in the studio the next day until three pm. After struggling to find the place, to our amazement it turned out to be above the strip club we had visited the night before!

That day we laid down two tracks. The session musicians were amazing and it was a really good experience, though not as glamorous as Miami as the studio was a bit rough and smelt of weed. The tracks we put down were 'Got to Get You into My Life' and 'Love You More Today than Yesterday', and we flew back to the UK with both of these now in our possession. Steve is friends with friends of Luke Goss (English actor / singer), who is married to Shirley Lewis, sister of the famous singer Linda Lewis and connected to the music industry though family and friends. Shirley sent the demos out to the record labels and Steve and I just waited for a response. The initial feedback was positive.

As soon as we came back from New York I had to do some filming for 'Seven Days With', a programme shown on the new channel ITVBe that followed my life for seven days - times with Emma and Harry life at home and what things were like being me. In my view it didn't show what my life was like at all! It was very staged and nothing was natural, but this was TV and it paid the bills.

Shortly after this Shirley Lewis got in touch, with the news that Warners had said they got me and what I was about. They were interested, but asked for one of the tracks to be reproduced. Naturally Steve wasn't happy, as we would have to go back to New York to re-record. He told me I'd have to go on my own, as I only had to put the vocal down and I didn't need him for that. For him this was a pain: flying me back to New York and sticking me in a hotel at the last minute wasn't cheap and not what he'd budgeted for. Meanwhile I did a lot of moaning to Emma about how much I needed Steve with me in New York. The upshot was that during a teleconference just before the trip Emma jumped in and told Steve - and not in the most tactful way! - that he should go with me, and after much deliberation and pleading he agreed. We re-did the track and it was good to have Steve there, as he was a lot of help in the studio and helped me get the most out of my time there. But it was not all plain sailing in New York; we tried to set up a meeting with Warners but they kept putting us off, so one night we went out for a drink in an Irish bar and decided to go it alone. We would set up our own label.

After we arrived back in the UK Warners turned me down: they'd decided I would be too much of a punt. We had just spent a fortune on this demo and it felt like we had been led the merry dance - the usual story of everyone promising the earth, but never delivering. It seemed like we were always at the final stages of signing the big deal that never materialised, so here I was back at square one again. We were now on our own, and at this point Steve set up a corporate gig in Jersey and a photo shoot; it was from this shoot that the front cover of the EP and this book came. The Jersey gig was amazing! I had a 15 piece band and a standing ovation at the end: it was the best gig we had done that year. We had five tracks recorded, so we decided to release an EP, which was released on 17th September 2014 and called 'Old Soul, Young Blood.' It debuted No 2 in the iTunes Jazz Chart, and on the strength of that we did a mini tour around the UK. It was not the best tour though, as the promoter let us down and it cost me and Steve more money. I was starting to learn that this music business is a hard game, and that you can't trust anyone it.

Just before we got to our venue in Liverpool, the Cavern, they called to tell us they had only sold 80 tickets; if we didn't sell over 100, we would have to cancel and re-arrange the date. The promoter had advertised the gig, but the venue had not received any posters and there had been no PR at all. There was only a little sign outside, which relied on passing trade, so I had to go to Liverpool and promote my own gig with help of my mum and our Sue. I sent them a poster that I made up on my phone on an happ and I told them to print it off, and get 500 fliers and 12 posters made. I sent them the money, and we went around and promoted my own gig. I had to pull in all the favours I had, got on the radio, and had fliers and posters in all the theatres. As a result, we were a sell-out on the night! Of course, performing in the Cavern in Liverpool was great, as I was playing where the Beatles had played so many years ago. I'm proud to say I have a brick in the wall in the Cavern with my name on it. It was for being in the public eye and coming from Liverpool. I learnt a lot on this tour though, one thing being that you cannot always rely on the people you think will support you. The first time I played at the Cavern was on the back of X Factor and I didn't have to do anything for a sell-out gig. This time *I* had to make it happen; *I* had to put the hard work in to help promote my own tours and myself.

Steve's dad is suffering from Parkinson's. I met him when I was in Jersey and it was really sad to see Steve with a dad who did not even recognise or acknowledge him. This was the first time that I had seen anyone with the disease; I had heard about it, but never seen the devastating affect it could have on people. It was at this time Steve came out with the idea of releasing a charity single in aid of 'Parkinson's UK'. The single was released on the 10th December, 2014 and titled 'the Beauty of Who You Are.' It reached No 2 in the iTunes easy listening charts, and the charity had an overwhelming response to the song, with over 2000 emails talking about it, what I had done, and about how the track we had released was so fitting.

To raise money to help produce the new album and tour Steve suggested we set up a crowd funding to generate revenue. We used a company called Crowd Shed and set a target figure of £15K. Steve explained this would be a good way to raise money and also test the water to see what fans there were out there, and what support we would get. For the crowd funding I would mention people on Twitter and they would get personalised CDs and free tickets to gigs, meet and greets, up to the point where I would do a private gig for someone wherever they wanted for £2500. It was a big success and we hit the £15K after 60 days, reaching just over £22K, which amounted to 140% over subscribed. This had given Steve and me a lot of confidence for the future. The funding had given us total control over the album and our sound, which was something I'd never, ever had in the past.

For the new album 'This Time Round' we didn't even bother going to the labels - we knew what sound we wanted to create. We want to put this album out as a true reflection of who we are. If the labels are interested in what we have produced, then we're more than happy to discuss it with them, but *this* time I feel it will be more under our terms.

Through Shaun Hargreaves we met 'Troaka', with two amazing guys called Sam and Nad who have great experience in the industry and have worked with the likes of 'Hans Zimmer' to name but one. We now have a team of song writers and producers that are all there to support me, and the new sound we have produced is a Motown-funk-soul combo which will show off my new vocals at their best. The new single 'They Say Love' will be released on 23rd February 2015; it's an original song written by 'NC1', part of the team that is now with me producing and writing songs. One of the things Steve has taught me is to work out a plan and stick to it, no matter what it takes. I know that the people supporting me all have my true interests at heart, and are focused on the same end goal that we have all agreed to as a team.

This is the most excited I have been for years. I am now in full artistic control of what I do, and also have full control of the way things are done around me. Steve has taught me so much about business and its importance on the road to success, as well as helping me realise my true passion for music. I know now that you don't have to wait around for people to let you down. Go for it, and the only person who can let you down is yourself!

Afterword

I have been in the entertainment industry since the age of three: I have won dance competitions for my country; I have been a household name through my childhood role in Brookside; runner up for the X Factor, and then recorded a Platinum selling album. You would have thought all this would have given me the golden ticket in this industry, but I was always in the hands of others. My management teams would get me a part yes, but at the price of a high percentage of my earnings. I was part of the tired old conveyer belt that has people joining it every year, all jostling for the same hour or so in the limelight. When you put your life in the hands of others, you need to make sure that they have your interest as their top priority.

Writing this book has been an emotional journey: it has made me retrace my life and take stock of what I have done and who I have been. Looking back, I shudder to think how naïve I was in some respects, controlled and manipulated by others. Now that I have completed this stage of my journey and am about to start the next chapter, I feel stronger and more confident in facing the future. During the re-launch of my career you may well read all sorts of stories about me. Some may be true, some may be distorted, and some may be down-right lies.

But I am who I am now, and I have never been so driven. I'm still only 26, and I have a lifetime ahead of me!

The end of this chapter and the start of the next.

Special Thanks

I would like to thank all those people who have helped me, crossed paths with me or had a hand in helping me in my career to date.

***

A special thank you to my manager Steve Coxshall who opened my eyes to the industry, given me direction and focus and the ability to believe in myself and fight for what I want from life. You're like a brother to me mate, thanks for seeing what you saw in me that day and choosing to dedicate your time to me.

***

I would also like to thank Barbara Mills for her help and support over the years. A massive thank you to my fans that have stood by me from the early years to now, who have dedicated their time to my web sites, twitter accounts and much more. You guys have never let me down.

***

I want to thank all of my coaches, teachers, mentors who have taught me all I know which has seen me through all the challenges that have been put in front of me.

***

Lastly a big thank you to the people who have given me opportunities from which I have learnt a lot.

More Non Fiction Titles
from Percy Publishing

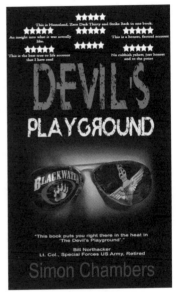

Out in April 2015

OUT NOW

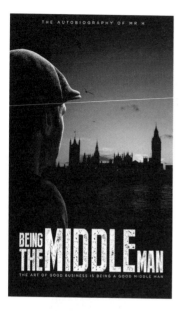

Out in May 2015

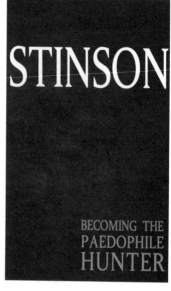

Out in June 2015

More Titles from
Percy Publishing Fiction

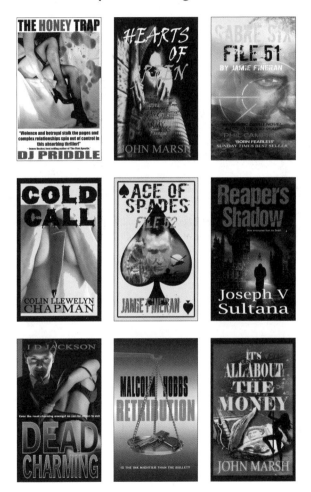

PERCY
PUBLISHING

Visit www.percy-publishing.com for more information.

Facebook: www.facebook.com/percypublishing

Twitter: @percypublishing

PR

Lucy Hilbert of Marker & Marker
www.markerandmarker.com

lucy.hilbert@markerandmarker.com